THOUGHTS, ANECDOTES AND STORIES FROM A PRIEST'S NOTEBOOK

– KENNETH PAYNE –

FASTPRINT PUBLISHING
PETERBOROUGH, ENGLAND

THOUGHTS, ANECDOTES AND STORIES FROM A PRIEST'S NOTEBOOK

ISBN 978-184426-590-9

First Published 2009 by

FASTPRINT PUBLISHING

Peterborough, England.

Printed on FSC approved paper by

www.printondemand-worldwide.com

CONTENTS

ACKNOWLEDGEMENTS

I am grateful for permission to reprint extracts from the following:

"The Zeal of Thy House" by Dorothy Sayers (David Higham Associates)

"Pastor Ignotus" in The Tablet, 29th September 2001

"Family Catechetics" April 1973 and article by Father Paul Edwards, June 1977 in the Clergy Review (now known as The Pastoral Review)

"Lightning Meditations" by Mgr. Ronald Knox (AP Watt Ltd on behalf of the Earl of Oxford and Asquith)

"Science and Christ" by Teilhard de Chardin (Science et Christ Oeuvres, tome IX © 1965)

In several cases I have been unable to trace the origin of a quotation and would be pleased to be informed so that in any further printing of the book the necessary permission may be obtained. Some of the names of people referred to, for obvious reasons, have been changed.

My especial thanks go to many, both mentioned and not mentioned, who have been a part of my life and an inspiration to me. I also extend my very special thanks to Lorna Foort for her help, encouragement, painstaking review and correction of the script, to Katherine Coburn for deciphering my scrawl and to Imre Balla for the cover photograph.

FOREWORD

Sometimes I am asked the question, "Why did you become a priest?" The usual, somewhat glib reply to that would be "Because God called me". However, penetrating deeper into this, I would say that it is because I have always had an urge, a desire, an impulsion, to spread the Good News I had been given on becoming a Catholic. Yes, and one could then say that this is itself God-given, God-calling.

My more recent urge to write has also been inspired by this desire to share the truth of Christianity and in particular, the very core of this truth, God himself. Increasingly in this multi-faith and at the same time Godless age, it seems to me important to appreciate more the mystery of love, and the mystery of God, The Trinity.

The first of these has recently been superbly dealt with by Pope Benedict in his first encyclical letter, "Deus Caritas Est", which is based on St John's words, "God is love, and he who abides in love abides in God, and God abides in him" (1 John 4 16).

The second mystery, God himself, is much more difficult to grasp – indeed, in many respects, impossible. God is love. "He" is one, true, good and beautiful, transcendent but at the same time immanent, active in the whole universe, and equally in the depths of each of us, and yet at the same time, unthinkable and unfathomable. Furthermore, having said that, side by side in each of us there are both elements of belief and acceptance as well as unbelief and questions.

How then, do we regard God, and in particular, the Christian Trinitarian God? Furthermore, how do, or how should, our lives revolve around our belief through worship and the daily routine of living?

I have tried to show in this very personal little book that God as a Trinity revealed by Christ does make sense and moreover, makes our Christian faith unique. This comprises the first and most important section of the book.

Subsequent Chapters are mostly anecdotes and stories, many of which are personal experiences from a fulfilled and happy life as a priest. They are both profound and light-hearted. The subjects covered are jottings from a notebook kept intermittently over the years. They complement an earlier book, "Shades of Welcome", and have been arranged in the form of different responses to God and his love. These are set out under the general headings of Jesus as the Way, the Truth and the Life, and this, I hope, makes reasonably coherent the seemingly disparate topics dealt with.

They include sections on prayer and retreat, the importance of space and leisure in our lives, guidelines to loving, our failures in this respect and finally, the change and rebirth that awaits us all in death.

Some of this will, I hope, make for amusing reading, but will in no way undermine the central thrust of the book which is to bear witness to the conviction that the Trinitarian God is at the centre of our lives and our world. He is all in all.

GOD AND HIS LOVE

Introduction and Some False Ideas

It is appropriate to begin this section on God with one of Father Anthony de Mello's stories:

Each day the disciple would ask the same question, "How shall I find God?"

And each day he would get the same mysterious answer, "Through desire."

"But I desire God with all my heart, don't I? Then why have I not found him?"

One day the Master happened to be bathing in the river with the disciple. He pushed the man's head under water and held it there while the poor fellow struggled desperately to break loose.

Next day it was the Master who began the conversation. "Why did you struggle so when I held your head under water?"

"Because I was gasping for air."

"When you are given the grace to gasp for God the way you gasped for air you will have found him."

Today, in what may be described as a Godless society, fewer people are gasping for God and even amongst those who do have faith there is a lack of appreciation of the revelation of God as a Trinity. It is this question that I wish to embark on at the outset.

G.K. Chesterton once drew a sketch of St Patrick, showing a man of enormous size with Chesterton, who was himself quite huge, standing beside St Patrick and in the picture looking minute. When thinking of writing about God, I feel like this, small and inadequate.

Society today bases many of its values on the material and technological, and yet the concept of a Being, a power beyond ourselves, is imbedded in all religion. Christians go a stage further and profess their belief in a Trinitarian God and in these days of inter-faith dialogue it is important and useful to delve a little into the meaning of this mystery and to see how it is linked with some of those fundamental questions we often ask: "What is life all about? Why are we here? and Why is there evil and suffering?"

I once, many years ago, had a conversation with a Muslim friend, who challenged me by saying: "God is one. Allah is one, so why do you complicate it by saying there are three Gods?"

"No," I replied, "not three Gods, but one God and three Persons......." I stopped, not sure how I would proceed. Indeed I wasn't sure what I really believed about the Trinity, and I was certainly unable to offer any explanation. A priest I knew once said that he was always glad when his first Holy Communion Sunday fell on the Feast of the Trinity because then he would not have to preach about it.

An atheistic Communist once knocked on a woman's door in Rome and tried to prove to her that there was no God. After some time he thought he had convinced her by his arguments until she waved her arms in the air and said, "All right, so there's no God! But there's always the Mother of God!"

And Lionel Blue tells the story of a Jew who was knocked over by a bus. A Catholic priest rushed over to him, bent down and asked, "Do you believe in the Father, Son and Holy Spirit?" The Jew opened his eyes and said, "I think I'm dying and you're asking me riddles!"

In a televised interview Joanna Rowlings, the authoress of the Harry Potter books, was asked, "Do you believe in God?", to which she replied, "Yes...yes, I think I do.....but it's difficult." However, later in the interview she described the Harry Potter books as the story of redemptive love. Yes, we might all agree that it is difficult, but if we speak of redemptive love we may well be on the way to appreciating something of the reality of God.

There are many who would like to believe in God and who would like to accept a power beyond themselves. Primitive man erected his totem pole which was a tribal symbol. It was something that could be seen and touched. A development of this is found in subsequent idols and representatives of a controlling power, controlling the weather and man's behaviour. For many today the term "god" suggests a first cause, a creator of the universe, of all that exists. When challenged, however, with the concept of a personal god, some would say that they would find this difficult to accept.

C.S. Lewis, in his book "Your God is too Small", enumerates several false images of God which many people have. Some are hangovers from childhood and others are partly derived from an incomplete and partial view held by the Israelites and others in Old Testament times. It will be useful to look briefly at them in order to clear our minds before moving on to the revelation of Christ.

a) God is like an old man beyond the clouds watching us in a benign way, but nevertheless remote and inaccessible.

b) In contrast to this is the image of God as a police officer controlling the speed cameras, a vindictive God.

c) Then there is the idea that God is like an all-embracive managing director. Inherent in this notion is that one cannot imagine how, with so many people to deal with, God could be interested in me! He is an impersonal God.

d) Because God is often addressed as "Father", there could be difficulties for those people who have had a difficult relationship with their own father, and hence they have a distorted concept of God.

e) Nor is God like an old-fashioned telephone operator, plugging in to each of our prayers and trying to deal in turn with our requests.

f) A further false idea is epitomised in the story of the small boy who was caught taking some chocolate biscuits from the tin.

"God will be angry with you for doing this.....just wait and see!" shouted his mother, who then sent him up to his room. Just then a violent thunderstorm broke out and when the lad's mother went upstairs to find him, she found him standing at the window eating the biscuits. "All this fuss", he said "about a few biscuits!"

And so one could go on... Many of these distorted notions of God are found in the thoughts of the Israelites before the coming of Christ. The revelation of Christ, that God is love and that he is Trinitarian was an enormous leap forward for many and was, as we shall see, only spelt out clearly in the early centuries of the Church's history.

Just as there were confusing and often false ideas of God before the coming of Christ, so there have been other distortions relating to the Trinitarian nature of God subsequent to Christ's revelation. Water, for example, can exist not only as water but also as ice or steam in different forms but each being H_20. Then some have compared the Trinity to an egg having a yolk, a white and a shell. A triangle and the three-leafed clover have also been used by way of illustration.

An extraordinary example can be seen in the Rushton Triangular Lodge, near Kettering and built in the late sixteenth century by Sir Thomas Tresham, the fruit of his meditations and study whilst in prison. Each of the three sides of the building within its three walls, three windows, three stories and three-sided chimney, relates to a Person of the Trinity. There are other reminders of the Trinity and also of the Mass; the chimney, for example, being set mysteriously above the centre of the building, its supports hidden – the mystery of faith.

More useful is the analogy used by the followers of St Athanasius who compared the Trinity to the light coming from the sun. At that time, of course, it was thought that the light was instantaneous, so that there was no delay between a ray of light leaving the sun and the time it struck the earth. The rays are derived from the sun and not vice versa. It is false to say that the sun existed first and then the light. The light is derived from the sun, but the light and the sun exist simultaneously throughout time. They are co-eternal – given the scientific knowledge of the time. Furthermore, we can know the sun only through the rays of light it emits. To see the sunlight is to see the sun.

Jesus himself commanded his followers to go and make disciples of all the nations, baptising them in the name of the Father and of the Son and of the Holy Spirit. (Matt 28_{19}). And on other occasions Jesus made the most extraordinary claims: "The Father and I are one" (John 10_{30}); "Anyone who has seen me has seen the Father" (John 14_{9}); "I am in the Father and the Father is in me" (John $14_{11)}$. It was through pondering on these and other words of Jesus that the Church formulated certain dogmatic statements spelt out as a result of various off-beat views of the nature of God and misinterpretations of passages in the Gospels.

One of the first of these was the Gnostic heresy. The adherents of this believed that salvation could be obtained through knowledge, and matter was hostile to spirit. God could not have become one with the human in Christ. Gnostics denied that Christ was truly man. This gave rise to the formulation of the Apostles Creed. Arianism, which developed in the fourth century, denied the divinity of Christ. God the Son did not exist from the beginning as part of the nature of God. Jehovah's Witnesses today follow Arius in claiming that Christ was not truly God.

The Nicene Creed to which the Orthodox, Catholics, Anglicans, Lutherans, Calvinists and many other Christian groups are committed, steers a way through both these heresies. However, it is important to fill it out, as it were, with the flesh. This is illustrated by the following story of a man who was questioning a recent convert to Christianity.

"So you have been converted to Christ?"

"Yes."

"Then you must know a great deal about him. Tell me: what country was he born in?"

"I don't know."

"What was his age when he died?"

"I don't know."

"How many sermons did he preach?"

"I don't know."

"You certainly know very little for a man who claims to be converted to Christ!"

"You are right. I am ashamed at how little I know about him. But this much I do know: Three years ago I was a drunkard. I was in debt. My family was falling to pieces. My wife and children would dread my return home each evening. But now I have given up drink; my children eagerly wait for my return home each evening. All this Christ has done for me. This much I know of Christ!"

We can know something about God through the signs of his presence:

Jim went to stay with his friend John, who, one night saw Jim praying. John remarked the following morning: "What's the use of that? How do you know there's a God? Have you ever seen God, heard him, touched him?"

"No," was the reply, "but there are signs of God all around us."

The next morning John informed his friend that the house had been burgled. "How do you know there's been a burglary?" asked Jim. "Did you see him, hear him, touch him?"

"No," replied John, "but the window was broken and the house in chaos...."

Nevertheless, having said that, it may also be claimed that between unbelief and belief there is a sort of no-man's land, and the less God is obvious, the more God is powerfully present. So, having left behind various aberrations of the notion of God, we can now move on to what I consider to be a most useful analogy, mentioned in the first place by St Augustine.

However, before doing just that it is appropriate to reproduce here the script of a talk I gave on the radio in Malta in 1958 whilst I was still a seminarian, preparing for the priesthood. I was surprised when re-reading it to realise that little of it has become dated.

Most of us, whether we are Catholic or non-Catholic, know the Beatitudes or counsels of good conduct that Christ gave us. G.K. Chesterton, that great English convert-writer, once suggested that there should be added another "Blessed is he that expecteth nothing, for he shall be gloriously surprised."

We all know the experience of planning and looking forward to a holiday. In our imagination we have enjoyed it even before it has taken place, and when the holiday actually comes, the reality so often proves different from what we had hoped: sometimes below our expectations, sometimes far above them.

Now, this philosophy of 'surprise' applies to the Catholic Faith as well as to the annual holiday. If we look at the Old Testament we see the Jews waiting for the Messiah – Yes, but not the sort of Messiah that Christ turned out to be! They certainly didn't expect God to be born of a woman at Nazareth ("Can anything good come out of Nazareth?" said one of the Jews.) That he should 'go through the mill' as it were – all the stages of growth and development that we ordinary humans experience, while still remaining God – that was the biggest surprise of all. A God-Man; he was completely and entirely God, and to appreciate that we have to rid our minds of all sorts of weird ideas of God that most of us have, thinking of Him as a sort of policeman, managing director, or an old man with a beard, and yet he was also completely and entirely man, virile and versatile, strong and courageous. If you had in mind the meek and mild dreamy type of individual, you should take another look at the Gospels. That this is what we mean when we talk about the Incarnation – God who became man by being born in the yard of an inn – that is the biggest surprise and the biggest mystery of all.

And it is precisely because the Christian Faith is based on this tremendous event – this 'surprise', that the whole gamut of truths bound up with this fact of a God incarnate is also pretty surprising, particularly to the outsider who first discovers or faces up to it. All those things which appear so odd to the non-Catholics, - praying in front of statues, kissing relics, bobbing up and down in front of the altar and so on – all these things seem as far removed from the fact that the Creator of all things became man as the actual coming of Christ must have seemed to those Jews who expected something rather different, even if they didn't quite know what it was that they did expect. And when we really meditate on the enormity of the fact of this God who became a Man, we begin to see that the Church he founded must, of necessity, be a mix-up of the spiritual and the material, the sacred and the profane. Just as God, in a sense, spiritualised the matter of his own body, so the spiritual should always permeate through and dominate over the material. But the non-Catholic, - what does he see? In a Catholic island like Malta, he soon becomes aware of the importance given to religion in the lives of the people. He is surrounded by churches and statues of the Virgin Mary. He sees people going in and out of church all day long. He sees processions with singing and shouting and gaiety – and bells ringing galore. What does he make of it all? So different from England, where religion is so often confined to going to Church on Sunday morning and where it makes little impact on the outsider. But what the non-Catholic visitor to Malta does not see is the spirit and attitude behind all this. He doesn't see into the mind of the man kneeling on the stone floor of the church in front of a highly coloured statue of the Virgin. He doesn't see that his reason for asking the Mother of Jesus to pray for him is because it was precisely in that way that the first miracle was performed when Jesus changed water into wine at the marriage feast at Cana. He doesn't see the sincere sorrow on the part of the man going to Confession, and the firm wish not to sin again, a wish of course that will never be totally fulfilled on this earth, since none of us is perfect.

The trouble in fact with most of us is, that at heart we are perfectionists. Worse still, we tend to think that only our own country, family, whatever it might be, can attain that perfection. This is pride and intolerance at its worst. We expect a person who goes to church to be perfect in all his, or her, actions outside church, and we are shocked and tend to say that religion is useless if a person goes to church in the morning and commits some act of vandalism in the afternoon. But Christianity is not only for the good, it is for the bad also, and we are all pretty poor or mediocre in one way or another, but the Church is there to help us to be better. It is a dreadful thing to look at others and expect them always to be perfect, without keeping a close eye on ourselves. This is probably one reason for the breakdown of many marriages: each one is looking for too high a degree of perfection in the other, and failing to find it, seeks elsewhere, with the same result. No! this is a world where, on account of man's sin, we are no longer perfect, and we must learn not to be surprised by the faults of our friends and relatives and acquaintances. And we can only do this by following Chesterton's dictum and expecting less of them in the first place, then perhaps we shall be pleasantly surprised by their good points.

Now, one big consequence of this element of surprise in religion and in life generally can be that we are more joyful and merry and happy if we accept and 'live' our religion; we can take an overall view of things; we can see more with the eyes of God than with our own limited and worldly vision. We can have a keener sense of humour. It's pretty certain that Christ Himself saw the funny side of things. Looking back on the account of his appearances after the Resurrection we see that the disciples at first failed to see the whole picture. Jesus' birth, life, death, resurrection and ascension all formed together a whole which was only appreciated years later. How amused Our Lord must have been when talking to the disciples on the road to Emmaus. They didn't recognise him and started telling him all about the events of the passion and crucifixion, and then the glorious surprise when they finally invited him to their house and recognised him in the breaking of bread.

The great tragedy is that we can easily lose sight of the complete picture, and by habit, become too used to the daily mundane things: the first time we ever drove a car; the first time we wore a dinner jacket or evening dress; the first time we saw the sun set at sea. All these were once new and carried with them an air of wonder and surprise, and then so quickly, we become accustomed to them all. We are then forced to the cinema or TV for new experiences and worlds to bring us quite unreal surprises – and that can be escapism.

We thrive on shock tactics. It's the unexpected and snappy answer that gets us. There is a story I like very much of the Jewish student who criticised a certain Rabbi for having given his last coin to a beggar, and the Rabbi's reply "Shall I be more particular than God who gave it to me?" That was a sort of shock treatment for the young student.

Our Lord gives us the secret of this philosophy of surprise when he says "Unless you become as little children you will not enter the Kingdom of heaven." Children are so often surprised by what to us adults is commonplace. So it is a childlike attitude that we need to have. G.K. Chesterton had this to an extraordinary degree, and it was this that gave him such an appreciation of what the church is. He always saw the forest, rather than the single tree or a withered leaf attached to it. He tells the story of the man who sat gazing at a spot on the carpet, and quite failed to see either the whole pattern on the carpet or the room or the house which contained it.

It is only by having this total view of religion and life that we can continue to keep alive our sense of wonder and our sense of humour. A belief in a personal Trinitarian God can help us do precisely this. But let us now move on to the great anology.

A Helpful Analogy

The inspiration for much of what follows was found in Dorothy Sayer's book "The Mind of the Maker", first published in 1941, and I am deeply grateful to her – a remarkable Anglican theologian who is, nevertheless, known more for her plays and detective stories than for her theology.

In her play "The Zeal of my House" she writes

"For every work [or act] of creation is threefold, an earthly trinity to match the heavenly.

First, [not in time, but merely in order of enumeration] there is the Creative idea, passionless, timeless, beholding the whole work complete at once, the end in the beginning; and this is the image of the Father.

Second, there is the Creative Energy [or Activity] begotten of that idea, working in time from beginning to end, with sweat and passion, being incarnate in the bonds of matter: and this is the image of the Word.

Third, there is the Creative Power, the meaning of the work and its response in the lively soul: and this is the image of the indwelling Spirit.

And these three are one, each equally in itself the whole work, whereof none can exist without the other: and this is the image of the Trinity."

And this is inspired by the words I once read, "when we become creative we approach holiness, wholeness – love". In her book "The Mind of the Maker", she expands on this theme and takes as her main example the mind of the writer of a book. The idea of a book is there in the author's mind; it then becomes 'incarnate', readable, seeable, touchable; and, if the work has been well-done, we can say that the author loves this "incarnation" of his or her idea. These three aspects of the human work of creation are an image, albeit an imperfect one, of the heavenly Trinity.

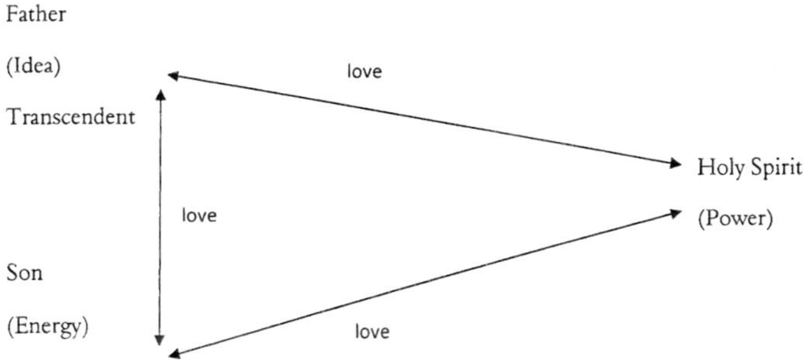

St Augustine wrote, "the image of the Trinity was made in man, that in this way man should be the image of the one true God."

Personally, I prefer the example of the artist who is painting a landscape. If he is a really good artist he will think first of the picture he wants to paint and will decide how to paint the lake, the background of trees and shadows, the boat on the lake and the fisherman. All this will be in his mind and he may tell his friends that he is going to paint a picture and describe it to them. They will then have some idea of what it is going to be like. He then sets about putting his idea on canvas. When completed, his friends will, he hopes, admire it, like it, love it, and say, "Ah, now we can see what you were describing to us: we can see the idea that was in your mind."

Here then, we have a clear Trinitarian image: the idea of the painting, and image of God, the Father; the approximate description of that idea before it becomes something tangible, is like the revelation of God to people before the coming of Christ, and the actual painting when completed, is an image of God, the Son, incarnation of the Father; and, finally the appreciation and love the artist and others have for the painting is an image of the Holy Spirit of love.

An even better Trinitarian image is found in the act of love between husband and wife. There is first of all, thought – perhaps sometimes an almost unconscious desire – on the part of the two people, which through intercourse, the act of love proceeding from each of them, may result in a third person. In this example we have a better image of the third 'person' of the heavenly Trinity.

However, this expression of love or image of the Trinity in our relationships is not limited to the family circle. It is found, or should be, in our relationships with one another. St Augustine said, "If you see love, you see the Trinity", or "Where there is love, there is God." The heart of the Trinity is love and the heart of love is the Trinity.

In God, of course, we are speaking of perfection. The first 'Person' of the Trinity utters his Word and externalises his thought and this is the Second Person of the Trinity, and they are bound for all time to each other by Love, the Holy Spirit. Here, we must always bear in mind that the word "Person" is not used in the Trinity in the way in which we normally use it.

However, not only do we find this trinitarian image in human acts of love and creation, but, to a lesser degree, in all our acts. Before we do anything there is the thought, the idea of doing it. It may be passing the salt at the dinner table or cleaning one's teeth or driving the car. The thought then becomes an action, it becomes incarnate, something seeable that can be experienced, the activity or energy. Then thirdly if we have acted well, there is the satisfaction, the love, the power between the thought and the action.

Many of the great saints have said that the smallest act done with love is of infinite value. Why is this? Simply, as we have just seen, it becomes a reflexion of the Trinity, and through it we are caught up in the movement of love that is God. I think it was Mother Teresa of Calcutta who remarked that we can do no great things – only small things with great love.

This, I would hasten to emphasise, is only an imperfect image of the heavenly Trinity, where time does not exist and so all three exist simultaneously. The Son is begotten of the Father from all time, before time began.

Mgr. Ronald Knox in his "Lightning Meditations" takes up this image in the Chapter, "Trinity Sunday" (page 70), where he writes – "When we speak so, we are no nearer to understanding the mystery. But man is made in the image of God, and perhaps it is some faint echo of everlasting truth, this desire of the artist to get hold of something which is 'part' of himself, and to externalise it."

On our human level, sin and imperfection in all that we do, mars the 'incarnation' of the idea in our minds. St Paul makes this plain when he writes, "I don't do the good I want to do; instead, I do the evil that I do not want to do." (Romans7$_{19}$) We never perform a perfect act and there are occasions when we actually go completely against love. The idea in our minds may be totally wrong or evil. It may become incarnate, but because it is intrinsically evil, there can be no movement of love between the idea and the action. Or more commonly, the 'action' is an imperfect showing forth of the idea in our mind.

Not only do we find this analogy in ourselves and the way we act, but we can apply it also to God and his creation – the creation of the whole vast universe, which is the "made material" of the initial idea in the mind of God. "And God saw all that he had made, and it was very good." (Genesis1_{31})

This leads me on to say a further word about the nature of love itself. We have seen that it is the Spirit of love that proceeds from the Father and the Son. Looked at from the angle of love itself, the Holy Spirit "looks" towards the Father and the Son: the Father, Pure Spirit, and the Son - incarnation, made flesh. We can then see how the Spirit, love, is derived from and directed towards the Father – and this is prayer. It is also derived from the Son and directed towards him and all creation – the good acts we perform for people and things.

One other fact needs to be added to this, namely that love invariably involves suffering, the cross. However this can lead to rebirth and new life. Even sin and evil can be turned to good given the right attitude of mind. In the Easter Liturgy we are reminded of that first act of rebellion of mankind – "O felix culpa", "O happy fault" that gave rise to the coming of a Saviour.

We have now seen how the creative activity of humans is trinitarian and a reflexion of the heavenly Trinity, and that the very core of this is love, just as it is in the heavenly Trinity. We have seen that this love always involves suffering and joy, death and life. On our human level it involves effort, work and often struggle, and on the heavenly level, God the Father becomes man who then goes to the limit of suffering, but it is followed by the peak of joy, of life in its fullest.

Before leaving this image of the Trinity, a word should be added regarding evil and sin. Jesus, on a number of occasions, spoke about sinning in one's thoughts. In one of the important summaries of his teachings Jesus, in the Sermon on the Mount, is teaching with authority, unlike the Scribes and the Pharisees. For them the Jewish law held the place of absolute authority. Jesus, however, quotes the law but then proceeds to contradict it and substitute his own teaching, cf Matthew $5_{21\text{-}43}$. The thrust of this teaching is that thoughts are as important as deeds and bad deeds as well as good deeds begin in the mind. Jesus is continually concerned with our thoughts.

How important it is, then, to fill the mind with good thoughts. One is reminded of the episode in J.M. Barrie's "Peter Pan": the children in their bedroom have seen Peter fly and they want to do the same; they have tried but failed. John asks, "How do you do it?", and Peter answers, "You just think lovely, wonderful thoughts and they lift you up in the air."

This is the way to defeat evil thoughts:

A great American football coach was asked once how it was he was so successful in training footballers and building up winning teams. He replied that it depended on how the footballer felt about the game and his fellow players. "In fact", he said "I would go so far as to say that I would not have a man in my team who did not have a genuinely friendly feeling for every other player in it. I have to get the most energy out of a man, and I have discovered that it cannot be done if he hates another man. Hate blocks his energy and he isn't up to par until he gets rid of it and develops a friendly feeling." (Source unknown)

Such is the power of thought, which may not be verbalised or "actionised", but nevertheless exists and may set up certain vibrations, "thought waves" and be on the way to becoming incarnate.

It also leads us on to ask why evil exists and what evil really is. If all that God created was, and is, good, how did evil come about? One approach to the answer to these questions is to say that it is the total absence of good, the negation of good. It is like asking the question, "Is the bung-hole part of the barrel?" - Yes, it is, but its reality is dependent on the reality of the barrel. Similarly "being" simply by existing creates "non-being" in both space and time.

Fear, and other allied emotions, is a lesser form of evil, a lack of love and trust. It wars against love and this is why it is the most frequent injunction on the lips of Jesus, "Do not worry.....", "Do not be afraid...." We so often experience fear of loss, fear of rejection, fear of alienation and that multitude of fears and worries and anxieties that invade our thoughts. But perfect love drives out fear.

Many will have seen some of those marvellous nature programmes with the commentary by David Attenborough. The amazing photography has captured some remarkable scenes in animal life especially that of predators, as well as on a lesser scale, in the life of birds, insects and sea creatures. In many of the scenes captured by the camera, I have been horrified by the cruelty and suffering involved. It seems to be built into nature itself.

Then one reflects on a no lesser cruelty and suffering that man inflicts on man: torture, warfare, terrorist attacks. And this is far worse since man is a superior and rational being not governed only be his instincts and lower desires. Man, by his very nature, is challenged to rise higher and beyond his animal nature. This is precisely what all great religious leaders have tried to show, and most of all, Jesus himself. Throughout his teaching he is calling us to be ruled by unselfish love, rather than by fear and hate.

Before leaving this section, it might be useful to mention that a few Christians in recent years have objected that expressing the Trinity as "Father, Son and Holy Spirit" is too male-orientated. Instead they would express it as "Creator, Redeemer and Sanctifier". This is an unnecessary complication, as for one thing, it overlooks the relational aspect of the heavenly Trinity and fails to highlight the oneness of the Trinity. Furthermore, in suggesting that it is a formula to be used in Baptism, it ignores the clear instruction and revelation of Jesus, that the dynamic nature of God is love, and that baptism should always be in the trinitarian form: "Go, and make disciples of all nations, baptizing them in the name of the Father, and of the Son, and of the Holy Spirit". (Matt 28_{19})

A further thought comes from Father Paul Edwards in an article in the Clergy Review back in 1977 when he writes:

The World Today, Image of God

Just when the world seems to be saying "Why discuss the Trinity – it's incomprehensible", we seem to have in the secular sciences a much deeper study of what is involved in being a relational being. We should say, a being made in the image of a God who is not just One, but also Three. No other God would serve modern man. All his strivings for Unity and Personality, for dependable, loving relationships, for Equality, Sharing, Communicating, all are found in the God from whom he came. Was there ever a time we knew so much about the Trinity from the study of ourselves? You could go on with every other human value we have come to see as more important as we have come to understand human nature more deeply. Perhaps I should not have left out Freedom, for after all the image of God in ourselves is a portrait we have to paint ourselves even if the paint and the canvas is provided.

If the best teacher is example, the Trinity itself would seem to offer the world all that it is seeking. May we find ways to direct its attention to the God who inspires the world's progress, but isn't getting the credit.

A more homely, moving and personal presentation of God, the Trinity, is to be found in William Young's spiritual novel, "The Shack". I have found this a thought-provoking, inspiring and devotional book, highlighting the importance of forgiveness and reconciliation in overcoming all evil. It complements my own thoughts about the Trinity as a loving relationship which should find a place in all our human relationships.

Jesus, the incarnate God, shows us the Way, the Truth and the Life – and this is what I will now consider.

OUR RESPONSE TO GOD

The Way of Prayer

A The Trinity and Prayer

Our first response to God and his love must be that of prayer – silence – contemplation – awareness, and so this section looks at a few aspects of this vast topic. I would emphasise that what follows are just a few jottings on the subject of prayer and in no way a treatise on the subject.

It is not only in acts of kindness and love, nor in the multitude of other activities of our daily lives where we reveal an image of the Trinity, but, first and foremost, in prayer. The time given to prayer each day, each week, is so important, as it is from this and through this, that our trinitarian activity derives. The composer, Judith Weir claimed that creativity is akin to meditation. When we pray we often fail to refer to or think of which of the three Persons of the Trinity we are addressing. They become somewhat vague and nebulous, and in a way one may think that this hardly matters. After all, all three are God.

However, many of the more formal prayers of the liturgy are usually addressed to the Father, through the Son and by the power of the Holy Spirit. This should remind us that, in prayer, we are truly caught up in this movement of love within the Trinity.

★ ★ ★

B Awareness

We may decide to set aside a certain time for prayer and then, having settled down to this, we find that boredom sets in. We find we are looking at the clock and thinking of the next thing to do, or we become anxious and worried about something that has happened in the past or may happen in the future. Instead, we have to crash through this stage of boredom, of distraction and the awareness of the passing of time, and instead, sink into an awareness of the present moment.

This can be done in a variety of ways, but one of the best is the simple awareness of our breathing. Without breathing any differently we become aware of the air passing through our nostrils, into our lungs, and out again. Or, as an alternative to this, an awareness of the sounds around us, or again, by just looking through the window and being aware of the countryside, the garden, the adjacent buildings or the passing people and traffic.

Contemplative prayer can be as simple as spending time just looking, listening, touching, smelling or tasting, and being aware of these sensations. Look at a tree – just look without wondering what sort of a tree it is, or how old it may be. Let the tree have an effect on you- just being aware of it. Similarly with listening to a bird or eating an orange - awareness.

God surrounds us, and is within us, rather like the atmosphere and the air we breathe. We are normally unaware of sound and sight waves around us except by means of the proper channels. Similarly we do not tune in to "God's waves" when there is no silence in our lives.

God is everywhere, but we can only tune into him if we move into silence and this is done by our awareness in the present moment. "Be still and know that I am God".

There are occasions in daily life when we are unaware, unobservant, and others, when we are fully aware of our surroundings. Another of Father de Mello's stories illustrates this:

A famous Viennese surgeon told his students that a surgeon needed two gifts: freedom from nausea and the power of observation.

He then dipped a finger into some nauseating fluid and licked it, requesting each of the students to do the same. They steeled themselves to do it and managed it without flinching.

With a smile, the surgeon then said, "Gentlemen, I congratulate you on passing the first test. But not, unfortunately, the second, for not one of you noticed that the finger I licked was not the one I dipped into the fluid."

Awareness is so important and is the beginning of contemplation and prayer. Indeed it should be the beginning of all activity.

* * *

C Other ways of praying

Having said that, we must not exclude other, shall I say, more sensory ways of communication with God and of him communicating with us. There is his word in Scripture, his Real Presence in the Eucharist, his look in the smile of a stranger, his action in the compassion shown by someone, and his touch in the loving hug of a friend.

Many young people want to find God, to experience something of God, and the voice of God is found, as we have seen, in silence, and this is helped through the use of subdued lighting and meditative music. This is one of the helpful aspects of the times of prayer at Taizé, which attracts so many thousands of young people – and the not so young. Prayer at Taizé not only involves periods of silence, the use of music, lighting and visual aids, but it occurs three times a day, morning, midday and evening. During prayer in the morning, soon after awakening, one's thoughts can be anticipating the happenings of the day, greeting them joyfully, with acceptance and hope. Then there comes the incarnation of those thoughts – of activities punctuated with a boost at midday and followed, at the end of the day, with a review of what has happened accompanied by thanksgiving, and where necessary, repentance.

However, much of our prayer time is too often taken up with asking. Intercession for others is important and necessary; petition for others and even ourselves may also be good. However, we should beware of ordering God to do this or that – and I am afraid that many of the prayers set out in the Roman Breviary and even in the liturgy of the Mass do just that. Our attitude should be that of abandonment: "I abandon myself into your hands, Lord. Do with me, and with others, what you will – your will, Lord, not mine, be done."

* * *

D Liturgical Prayer

Ancient Greek buildings can be Doric, Ionic or Corinthian. Byzantine walls are often an utter shambles as architecture deteriorated from Greek to Roman to Byzantine, the last building their walls out of odd bits of stone and anything else they could find. Design became in some aspects less haphazard when in the west, it developed into Norman and Gothic.

Bourges Cathedral in France has no transepts to break up the magnificent lines of the interior Gothic which soars upwards, as it were to God. Romanesque (Norman) is centred more on the altar and the interior with its rounded arches. Hence the former is somehow symbolic of external praise of God in singing and vocal prayer, whilst the Norman suggests more the interior life and finding God within. We must remember that liturgical prayer should be tempered by our human situation.

One Christmas Eve I was unexpectedly asked by a priest in a village some twelve miles away to celebrate an early 'midnight' Mass as he wasn't feeling well. I made a quick calculation that it would still leave me time to return to celebrate the Vigil and Mass at midnight in the Cathedral.

As I left Northampton fog descended and soon became thick and freezing. I was not too sure of my route and contemplated phoning and turning back. It was then that I remembered that it was on Christmas Day, the first anniversary of Bishop Frank Thomas' death. I uttered a prayer to him – and quite suddenly there was a change. The following day I recounted this to another priest. "What happened?" he asked, "Did the fog lift?"

"No", I replied, "the fog didn't change but I changed, and quite suddenly my whole attitude and fear was transformed into trust and confidence: yes, I could go on and all was well." Over two hundred people had ventured out for the Mass, and by the time I had finished, the fog had, in fact, cleared and I was in good time back at the Cathedral. Prayer can change us.

* * *

Popular religion impregnating typical joyful Mauritian disorder would probably best describe the priestly ordination of a friend on the island of Mauritius in the South Indian Ocean. There were about ninety concelebrating clergy and a congregation of over twenty thousand people gathered on the hillside leading up to the altar of Marie Reine de la Paix. Heavy clouds also gathered in the sky above and during the Litany of the Saints the rain commenced. The great crowd was suddenly enveloped under a multitude of coloured umbrellas and parasols.

The Gospel, which was the account of the marriage feast at Cana, was sung by a young priest in Creole, and he punctuated it with the refrain, also in Creole, "Do whatever he tells you." It was very moving.

After the ordination I found myself chatting to a number of people, amongst whom was a priest from Belgium and several from France, a little Brother of Jesus, a priest from Ireland, and a couple who had come from France specially for the ordination, combining it with a holiday. They remarked that in their travels all over Europe they had never encountered such openness and hospitality as they had experienced since arriving in Mauritius. With this I totally agreed.

* * *

The Bishop returned from a Low Week meeting exclaiming that he had learned the difference between a terrorist and a liturgist: a terrorist you can argue with but a liturgist you can't!

This reminded me of an event in 1971 when I had encouraged Gordon Rock to take part in a Folk Music weekend at Wood Hall in Yorkshire. Gordon, during the weekend, was inspired to set the creed to music. Five days later he had written the whole of the Mass, which was published by Kevin Mayhew and known as the Pilgrim Mass. However, it later ran into trouble as the liturgists objected that it had not kept strictly to the official translation of the Mass.

It may have been an attempt to prevent me from raising my voice over matters liturgical, that a few years later I was made chairman of the Diocesan Liturgy Commission – until about 1980 when I resigned as I had accumulated too many extra-parochial jobs. Father John Glen took over from me until he died subsequent to a fire in his presbytery.

Liturgical norms were also slightly stretched when in 1988 we had a Service of Reconciliation with General Absolution in Northampton Cathedral. The bishop had agreed that it would be good to have this occasionally. The Cathedral was packed to the porches, and it was clearly greatly appreciated. I made the point in the homily that it was to emphasise the communal aspect of sin and forgiveness, and should always point to individual and private confession.

⋆ ⋆ ⋆

At the conclusion of the final Mass of an ecumenical visit to Poitiers, Northampton's twin town, and following on a fanfare of trumpets and flag and banner waving, I thanked everyone for such a wonderful welcome, at which the Bishop took me by the arm and whispered to me that I couldn't really have quite the last word, but he would let me take part in the last gesture. "Come", he said, "and give the blessing with me", and so I found myself giving the triple episcopal blessing.

⋆ ⋆ ⋆

Many of the psalms – but by no means all of them – mean little to me as a form of prayer, and this causes me to be very selective in using the breviary. Their background culture is different, they are often expressions of human anger and hatred and even attach these emotions to God himself. I have only twice found an echo of these thoughts openly expressed.

The first was some years ago when I was seated on the rocks near the jetty at Kyrenia on the north coast of Cyprus reading Bede Griffiths book "Creation in Christ" and I nearly stood up and cried out with enthusiasm when I found him stating that the problem of the psalms was becoming acute and the psalter needed to be revised. Some psalms and certain verses, he thought, should be omitted because they are really scandalous and he concludes that we should learn to read or sing the psalms with more discrimination.

Secondly, this is exactly what is done in the daily prayer at Taizé in which a few selected verses are sung and many short psalm or biblical phrases are set to music as a repetitive chant or mantra.

⋆ ⋆ ⋆

It is important to understand the significance of ritual. Two nuns were involved in the organisation of a 1,800 strong high school in Kingston, Jamaica and Sister James explained that the whole school never got together for an assembly as there were too many of them. There were 102 on the staff and 5% of the children were Catholic, although about 50% were baptised. However, at the beginning of the semester Sister James thought it important to have the school blessed.

I was asked to do this, and it consisted of a short service of blessing of the water in the school office. This was relayed to all the classrooms. Some children gathered around me to sing a hymn and three were by me with medium-sized plastic buckets of water to be blessed. I wondered whether I was supposed to drench the children as I went around to the different classrooms, bearing in mind that Jamaicans, if they experience a drop of rain, hide indoors! In one classroom the spongy end of the sprinkler I was using detached itself and shot across the room, fortunately not hurting anyone, but causing a roar of laughter.

In spite of saying a few words in each classroom, I had the impression that not many appreciated what it was all about. I think we have to be careful and selective in the outward expressions of our faith.

⋆ ⋆ ⋆

One Sunday I was celebrating Mass at Faith Centre in down-town Kingston, Jamaica, the congregation being made up of some of the Missionaries of the Poor Brothers, residents at the Centre and a crowd who had come in from the surrounding slums. All sang enthusiastically accompanied by two Brothers on various instruments. The homily was well received with lots of "Praise the Lords and Amens" and nodding of heads.

After Mass one lady came up to me and asked me to bless her eye which was giving trouble. This I did, and immediately someone else came up with another pain and I prayed over them. In no time at all there was a queue of probably about 40 people who wanted to be prayed over and so I was standing outside the church by this time as one of the brothers was taking a catechism class inside and standing in the increasingly warm sun. They all came up to me explaining what was wrong and wanting to be prayed over. It was really quite a moving experience and seemed to be very much appreciated. I didn't realise until afterwards that Brother Max and several other brothers were very patiently waiting for me in the car. I apologised and Brother Max said "Well it's all right as long as it doesn't happen every Sunday!"

* * *

E Good Example

At the monthly Taizé style prayer at the Cathedral in October 1996 we followed it, as usual, with a simple shared supper. On this occasion there were about eighteen of us around the table. At one point Roger Sawtell, who coordinates the group, banged the table to get silence and announced that about fifteen months ago a nephew of his, Peter Brown, quite a young child, had been ill with a hole in his heart and various complications. He had been admitted to hospital and Roger had asked the Taizé group to pray for him. Later that same evening Roger had gone upstairs in Cathedral House to where my father resided and had told him about the young lad. My father had promised to pray for him too. Roger then went on to relate that he had just spoken with my father again, fifteen months later, and the latter had asked Roger how Peter was, saying that he had been praying for him regularly during that time. The boy had recovered, the rest of us had almost certainly forgotten the prayer request, except my father, who at the age of 97, had remembered.

* * *

At Woking County Grammar School Speech Day on 26th November 1948, Admiral of the Fleet, Lord Tovey distributed the awards and made a short speech. He said that, in spite of causing disappointment because he was not going to tell the usual amusing anecdotes of his experiences, he thought it necessary to speak on a more serious subject. He felt that the present condition of the world could in large be remedied if a greater consideration was given to religion. He emphasised the importance of prayer and mentioned a few of his own experiences where he found miracles performed by his application of prayer. In a trying moment, he said, he would go to his cabin and get down on his knees and send up a prayer to God. It was wonderful how relieved and what confidence he had on getting up again. Many men, the ordinary sailors, had no cabins to retreat to, and they spent their time forever in others' company. A prayer, however, he said was still possible.

* * *

It is important that we give time for prayer.

There are 168 hours in each week:
56 in sleep
48 to work
12 for meals
52 hours left
A tithe of 1/10 of this would be 5.2 hours.

I hour for Mass each week leaves 252 minutes. Which is over 30 minutes each day and still plenty left over for chores and fun!

* * *

I was introduced to the importance of prayer by my grandmother who died in May, 1954. The sun shone brightly as her tired body was lowered into the earth at Burnham-on-Crouch cemetery. I felt that she was looking on at her funeral and was pleased with the flowers and the weather.

I remembered how, one day, when she was staying with us at Jacobswell, Mr Ackermann, my Godmother's husband, came into the lounge and found Grandma on the floor, having just fallen, and how Grandma laughed about it afterwards.

One afternoon she went out by herself and was away for more than two hours – much to my Mother's consternation. She had walked to St Edward's church at the top of the nearby hill, and sat in the church for over an hour. She had considerable sympathy with the Catholic faith, although she hadn't known that her father had been a baptised Catholic.

She must have been unutterably lonely living in the bungalow at Burnham with the armchair opposite empty.

For me that bungalow, "Glenroy", Mill Road, was more of a home than anywhere else. The furniture was always the same; nothing ever changed. The settee, under which I can remember pushing my toys when I lived there for over two years whilst Mother was in hospital with TB, was always in the same place.

Grandma used to take me for walks and when we passed a telegraph pole and heard the humming of the wind in the wires, she would say that was Mother sending me a message – and she would tell me what the message was. In that way and in so many others she kept vividly before me the memory of Mother.

I can remember lying in my bedroom at Burnham sobbing for hours a night because Mother was ill, and through Grandma I had a complete and absolute faith that "Jesus would make Mummy better" – and he did.

It is now a very beautiful memory: like a poem, with the tremendous love that my Grandparents had for each other, their great faith in God and their simplicity of life.

* * *

To prepare to take part in one of Don McClean's programmes on Radio 2 on a Sunday morning, I was invited to dinner at a nearby hotel to discuss plans for the following day as it was to take place during the annual Balloon Festival and I was to speak about the Missionaries of the Poor. Eleven of us gathered for the meal, broadcasters, technicians, producer, BBC crew, etc. Before we sat down Denis Nowlen turned to me and said, "Father Ken, would you lead us in the Grace?" Immediately the whole group joined hands, whilst other people in the crowded restaurant turned to look as we prayed together for a moment or two. It was a great witness to faith.

⋆ ⋆ ⋆

I was invited to a great family gathering in Mauritius. I was asked to lead the prayer before we sat down. As soon as I'd finished a young wife burst into song, quite spontaneously, a song of prayer and praise. Over the meal conversation turned to the Gospel that had been read at Mass that morning. There ensued a very natural and unselfconscious sharing of what the Lord was saying to us in several passages. All were very committed to their faith. Mauritians are, in fact, reputed to be committed to three things: their religion, eating and drinking, and the sea!

⋆ ⋆ ⋆

I began this section on prayer mentioning the importance of awareness, and it is appropriate to end with another of Tony de Mello's stories, which sums it up:-

The temple had stood on an island two miles out to sea. And it held a thousand bells. Big bells, small bells, bells fashioned by the best craftsmen in the world. When a wind blew or a storm raged, all the temple bells would peal out in unison, producing a symphony that sent the heart of the hearer into raptures.

But over the centuries the island sank into the sea and with it, the temple and the bells. An ancient tradition said that the bells continued to peal out ceaselessly, and could be heard by anyone who listened attentively. Inspired by this tradition, a young man travelled thousands of miles, determined to hear those bells. He sat for days on the shore, opposite the place where the temple had once stood, and listened – listened with all his heart. But all he could hear was the sound of the waves breaking on the shore. He made every effort to push away the sound of the waves so that he could hear the bells. But all to no avail; the sound of the sea seemed to flood the universe. He kept at this for many weeks. When he got disheartened he would listen to the words of the village pundits who spoke with unction of the legend of the temple bells and of those who had heard them and proved the legend to be true. And his heart would be aflame as he heard their words... only to become discouraged again when weeks of further effort yielded no results.

Finally he decided to give up the attempt. Perhaps he was not destined to be one of those fortunate ones who heard the bells. Perhaps the legend was not true. He would return home and admit failure. It was his final day, and he went to his favourite spot on the shore to say goodbye to the sea and the sky and the wind and the coconut trees. He lay on the sands, gazing up at the sky, listening to the sound of the sea. He did not resist that sound that day. Instead, he gave himself over to it, and found it was a pleasant, soothing sound, this roar of the waves. Soon he became so lost in the sound that he was barely conscious of himself, so deep was the silence that the sound produced in his heart.

In the depth of that silence, he heard it! The tinkle of a tiny bell followed by another, and another and another... and soon every one of the thousand temple bells was pealing out in glorious unison, and his heart was transported with wonder and joy.

If you wish to hear the temple bells, listen to the sound of the sea.

If you wish to see God, look attentively at creation: don't reject it; don't reflect on it; just look at it. Silence alone brings transformation....."Wherever you may be, look when there is apparently nothing to see; listen when all is seemingly quiet."

This approaches the experience of eternity which may be described as pure presence – living totally and fully in the present moment – the sacrament of the present moment.

The Way of Retreat

A day's retreat which could be attempted on one's own

(a) Choose a passage from Scripture. The following is taken as an example.

A Reading from St Paul's letter to the Philippians. 4:4-7, 11-13

May you always be joyful in your union with the Lord. I say it again; Rejoice! Show a gentle attitude towards everyone. The Lord is coming soon. Don't worry about anything but in all your prayers ask God for what you need, always asking him with a thankful heart. And God's peace, which is far beyond human understanding, will keep your hearts and minds safe in union with Christ Jesus.....

I have learnt to be satisfied with what I have. I know what it is to be in need and what it is to have more than enough. I have learnt this secret, so that anywhere, at any time, I am content, whether I am full or hungry, whether I have too much or too little.

I have the strength to face all conditions by the power that Christ gives me.

★ ★ ★

(b) It is useful to know something of the background to this extract. Paul wrote this letter from prison in Rome, and he was clearly reminded of his stay in Philippi when he had also been imprisoned.

Philippi was a great commercial centre in the ancient world, renowned for its gold and silver mines. It had been founded by Philip, the father of Alexander the Great, in the fourth century, and it overlooked the trade route between Europe and Asia.

In AD52 Paul visited it on his second missionary journey; read Acts 16. It was there that he was instrumental in the conversion of three very different people: Lydia, who was Asiatic and a wealthy woman in the purple dye trade; a Greek slave girl at the bottom of the social ladder, and the Roman gaoler when he was put in prison for his outspokenness.

These, and many others, would be the recipients of his letter.

★ ★ ★

(c) Ponder on a few words in the letter calling to mind what they might mean for oneself. The words taken for the sake of these examples are underlined in the text.

Joyful   Joy is a word very frequently used in this letter. It means a deep happiness and contentment. Are we joyful in our following of Christ and spreading our faith and love? (Phil $1_{18,25}$) And even when we suffer? (Phil 2_{17}) or show hospitality? (Phil 2_{29}) The Blessed Mother Teresa once said that "a joyful heart is the normal result of a heart burning with love".

<u>Gentleness</u> Does this tie up with our attitude to other people? Are we gentle in our dealings with one another? In the marriage service both bride and bridegroom are asked to cherish each other. This is a beautiful English word meaning not only to love but to care for, look after, to protect and keep safe. All these attributes could be included under the heading of "gentleness".

<u>Worry</u> For the Christians in Philippi it must often have been a source of worry and anxiety just being known as a Christian. What do I worry most about? In the end, what difference does it make? Jesus' most frequent command was "do not worry", "do not be afraid", "fear not".

Worry denotes a lack of trust and ultimately, a lack of love.

We need to drop our attachments and worries, which are like clouds in the sky, and identify with the blue sky, being able then to say, without alarm, "Ah, here comes a cloud!"

Even when it comes to reflecting on our sins, we should not worry, but rather, remind ourselves of the love and mercy of God when we truly repent. It is usually good to reflect for a short while on one's failings, not in the sense of compiling a "shopping list" of sins, but of seeing the ways in which one has blocked God's flow of love and life through our waywardness, and, yes, through our failure to trust.

<u>Prayer</u> It is always good at a time of retreat to reflect on how one prays. St Paul, in this letter, makes the point that prayer should be basically infused with thanksgiving and intercession. Let us, then, remind ourselves of a few of the many ways of praying, bearing in mind the dictum, "pray as you can and not as you can't".

- Set prayers, as in the liturgy or to be found in a suitable prayer book: these can be helpful but their meaning must respond to one's inner thoughts and feelings.
- The Rosary is like a song with a rhythmic accompaniment. The meditation on one of the events in the life of the Lord, or in the case of two of them, of Our Lady, can be likened to the words of the song, whilst the Hail Marys correspond to the beat of the accompanying music. It is often helpful to go a step further and remind oneself that Christ continues to be born, live, suffer and die today in those around us. For example, for the fourth joyful mystery, the Visitation, one could link with prayer for a safe journey as a Christ-bearer, or in the third sorrowful mystery, the Crowning with Thorns, prayer for those, especially those who are mentally disabled.
- Another sort of "rosary" is what I call the hand rosary. This can be helpful when just walking along the road or waiting in a queue. Each finger becomes a reminder of a person or group of people to remember in prayer, the left

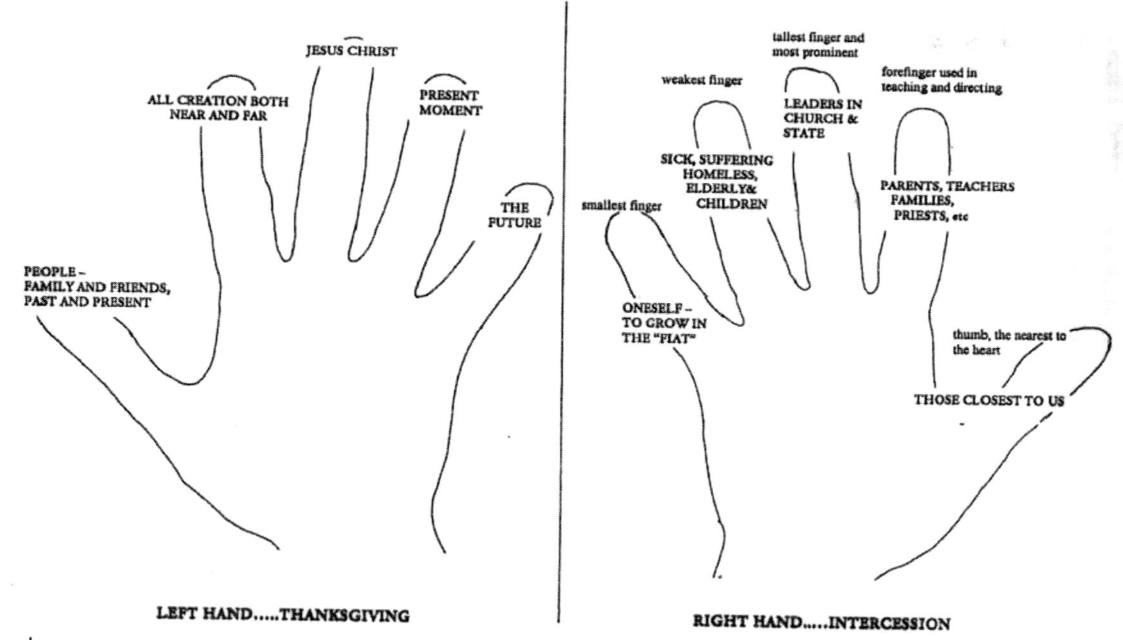
THE HAND ROSARY
JESUS CHRIST
ALL CREATION BOTH
NEAR AND FAR
PRESENT
MOMENT
THE
FUTURE
PEOPLE –
FAMILY AND FRIENDS,
PAST AND PRESENT
LEFT HAND.....THANKSGIVING
tallest finger and
most prominent
weakest finger
forefinger used in
teaching and directing
LEADERS IN
CHURCH &
STATE
SICK, SUFFERING
HOMELESS,
ELDERLY&
CHILDREN
smallest finger
PARENTS, TEACHERS
FAMILIES,
PRIESTS, etc
ONESELF –
TO GROW IN
THE "FIAT"
thumb, the nearest to
the heart
THOSE CLOSEST TO US
RIGHT HAND.....INTERCESSION

hand being that of thanksgiving and the right hand that of intercession. The previous sketch illustrates this. A prelude to a more contemplative style of prayer can be that of kneeling or sitting with one's back straight (not in an armchair!) and just listening or looking, or being aware of one's bodily sensations, or, perhaps best of all, as previously mentioned, aware of one's breathing - doing nothing else but that: awareness. This leads naturally into contemplation; indeed, it is contemplation and from this one can slide simply into the use of a mantra: a single word, "maranatha" (Come, Lord), or the Jesus prayer which is popular amongst Orthodox Christians: "Jesus, Son of God, Saviour, have mercy on me, a sinner". This can, of course, be shortened, even to the one word, "Jesus".

- We should, then, be moving away from the idea that prayer is just a question of "asking" – ask, yes, as St Paul says, but with a thankful heart, and, even then there is really just one "thing" that, before all else, we should ask for, and that is illustrated by the Eastern story of the Lord Vishnu:

The Lord Vishnu was so tired of his devotee's constant petitions that he appeared to him one day and said: "I have decided to grant you any three things you ask for. After that, I shall give you nothing more."

The devotee delightedly made his first petition at once. He asked that his wife should die so that he could marry a better woman. His petition was immediately granted.

But when friends and relatives gathered for the funeral and began to recall all the good qualities of his wife, the devotee realised he had been hasty. He now realised he had been quite blind to all her virtues. Was he likely to find another woman quite as good as her?

So he asked the Lord to bring her back to life! That left him with just one petition. And he was determined not to make a mistake this time, for he would have no chance to correct it. He consulted widely. Some of his friends advised him to ask for immortality. But of what good was immortality, said others, if he did not have good health? And of what use was health if he had no money? And of what use was money if he had no friends? Years passed and he could not make up his mind what to ask for: life or health or wealth or power or love. Finally he said to the Lord, "Please advise me on what to ask for."

The Lord laughed when he saw the man's predicament and said, "Ask to be contented no matter what life brings."

"Peace of mind, no matter what happens", and this is precisely the gift of the Holy Spirit, and so we pray, "Come Holy Spirit, fill our hearts............."

<u>Peace</u> To be a person infused with the gift of God's peace is one of the best advertisements for the truth of Christianity. So often we obliterate that peace by our tendency to complain and grumble. We become "doom and gloom" people. However, if we make the effort to live in the present moment – recommended by all spiritual writers – satisfied with what we have – or have not – then we will know that contentment and peace which comes "by the power that Christ gives us".

Pope John Paul II: "Duc in altum" "Put out into the deep".

These words invite us to remember the past with gratitude, to live the present with enthusiasm, to look forward to the future with confidence.

Prayer of Abandonment. (Charles de Foucauld)

Father, I abandon myself into your hands: do with me what you will. Whatever you may do I thank you: I am ready for all, I accept all. Let only your will be done in me, and in all your creatures. I wish no more that this, O Lord.

Into your hands I commend my spirit; I offer it to you with all the love of my heart, for I love you, Lord and so need to give myself, to surrender myself into your hands, without reserve, and with boundless confidence, for you are my Father.

The Power of Christ

Before concluding the notes for this retreat, it is good to be reminded that our prayer can first of all be directed, as we have seen, to God, the Trinity. However we should also address Jesus present in the Eucharist, which after all, is the continuation of the Incarnation, and lifts creation to its highest level.

In the Eucharist, Jesus is saying, "Take my life into the very centre of your being." Blood, for the Jews, is "liquid life", and for us, in the chalice of salvation, it is Jesus' life. When he enters into us we can feed upon his life and strength and vitality and be re-vitalised.

Spike Milligan once told an interviewer, "Though a Catholic, I never went to Holy Communion because it was too good, and I was too filthy." However, we all admit out unworthiness in the prayer before Communion.

From the sublime to the ridiculous, I was once visiting Bourges Cathedral, and on looking around failed to see a lighted sanctuary lamp indicating the Real Presence of Jesus in the tabernacle. On asking the sacristan where the Blessed Sacrament was reserved and why there was no light in front of the tabernacle, he replied, "Ah, mais ce n'est qu'une petite hostie!" ("Ah, but it is only a small host there.")

It was in March 1999 that, with a friend, I climbed steeply up a hill on the summit of which was the statue of Christ, the Redeemer. It was just outside Rio de Janeiro and although there was some mist about and low cloud, one could clearly see the statue on the top of the hill dominating

Rio. However by the time we had got to it, the whole summit of the hill, including the statue, was cloaked in whirling mist.

Quite a few people were there, mostly like myself with cameras waiting to take views of the statue and of the panoramic view of Rio itself. We waited for over half an hour, and then quite unexpectedly, for just a few moments, there was blue sky and sunshine and the mist had abated. However it was not for long and only a few of us who had been patient were rewarded with the sight of Christ looking down on us.

Perhaps life itself is a little like that: Christ just occasionally revealing himself in different ways to us.

* * *

The pelican was used in the Middle Ages as an image of Christ's love for us seen in the Eucharist. It was believed that whenever the pelican was unable to find enough food for her young she would bite off flesh from her own body in order to feed her babies, literally giving her life to her children....................Jesus says, "Eat my flesh...........drink my blood..........."

* * *

Then, finally, we have the whole Communion of Saints, headed in a unique way by Our Lady, whom we ask to join her prayers with ours. In the beautiful tenth century church of Saints Mary and Donato on the island of Murano in the Venetian lagoon there is an unusual mosaic of Our Lady. Her hands are facing outwards, in an attitude of prayer although her gaze is directed to the side, as if to indicate "not yet, but in God's good time".

May Our Lady lead us ever closer to her Son, the Way, the Truth and the Life.

⋆ ⋆ ⋆

For a longer retreat, extending, if one wished, to a week or even ten days, I can think of few better books to follow than Franz Jolics' "Contemplative Retreat – an Introduction to the Contemplative Way of Life and to the Jesus Prayer". It is published by Xulon Press, and available through Amazon.

Have a good retreat!

⋆ ⋆ ⋆

The Way of Leisure

We are often in danger of overlooking the fact that our response to God is not only in prayer, but in life itself, and even in our leisure activities, or in inactivity.

What is life if, full of care
We have no time to stand and stare.
No time to stand beneath the boughs
And stare as long as sheep or cows.
No time to see, when woods we pass,
Where squirrels hide their nuts in grass.
No time to see, in broad daylight,
Streams full of stars, like skies at night.
No time to turn at Beauty's glance,
And watch her feet, how they can dance.
No time to wait till her mouth can
Enrich that smile her eyes began.
A poor life this if, full of care,
We have no time to stand and stare.
[W.H. Davis]

⋆ ⋆ ⋆

Leisure, though, is not inertia, as shown in this improbable story.

A gentleman knocked on his son's door. "Michael" he said, "wake up!" Michael sleepily answered, "I don't want to get up, Dad." The father shouted, "Get up, you have to go to school," and Michael replied, "I don't want to go to school." "Why not?" asked the father. "Three reasons," replied Michael. "First, because it's so dull; second, the kids tease me; and third, I just hate school and I don't want to get up." And the father replied, "Well, I'm going to give you three reasons why you <u>must</u> go to school. First, because it's your duty; second, because you're forty five years old, and third, because you're the Headmaster." Wake up!

* * *

"Manâna" I'll do it tomorrow; or "soon come" are common expressions in some cultures. "Now", is the appropriate time. The past will never return and the future may never arrive. This may also be expressed by the saying that yesterday is history; tomorrow is a mystery; but today is a gift and that is why we call it – the present!

* * *

One day my father and I called on Bishop Charles Grant who was living in retirement in a small bungalow at Kiln Green, near Reading. All his needs were provided for by the nuns who lived in the nearby house.

At one point in the conversation my father turned to the bishop and enquired, "Bishop, what do you do all day?" To which Bishop Grant, who was lounging in his armchair puffing on a cigarette, smiled and replied “Nothing – and I enjoy it.”

* * *

In the early 1970s it was unusual for priests to have a beard. Canon Law had only just allowed it, and I was one of the first: I had always rebelled at the waste of time in unnaturally shaving each morning. When the opportunity arose I informed the Bishop that I now qualified for 4½ days and nights extra holiday each year, as this is what I saved through not shaving!

* * *

Being close to nature can help one to relax, and, when younger, I used to enjoy camping – which reminds me of what is said to be officially the funniest joke in the world. I include it for its own sake!

Sherlock Holmes and Dr Watson went camping and pitched their tent under the stars. During the night, Holmes woke his companion and said, “Watson, look up at the stars, and tell me what you deduce.” Watson replied, “I see millions of stars and, even if a few of those have planets, it’s quite likely there are some planets like Earth and if there are a few planets like Earth out there, there might also be life.” Sherlock Holmes replied: “Watson, you idiot. Somebody stole our tent...”

* * *

Laughter is a form of exercise which can infuse our work as well as our leisure. It is a sign of mental health. It releases endorphins and other hormones to the brain, increases circulation and lowers blood pressure. Time passes more quickly and mundane tasks seem easier. It releases the mind from depression. A recent study showed that roaring with laughter can boost the immune system by nearly 40%. Perhaps laughter should be regarded as a complementary therapy.

* * *

We all have hobbies or leisure activities which help us to relax and become more true to ourselves. For me, going to the theatre or a concert achieves this. At the end of a fairly arduous first term at the French Seminary of St Sulpice, with its attempts to understand the French language, three of us English students, (Monty White, Michael Richards and I), decided to relax as we were unable to get a boat back to England until the following day. We managed to get three tickets for "the gods" at the Grand Opera House in Paris.

Unfortunately Monty found himself in a seat which was jammed, and throughout the overture and part of the first number he was struggling with his seat to the accompaniment of increasing "tuts and shs" from the audience behind him. In the end I whispered to him to kneel down until the Interval which he finally did. I'm not sure whether I passed him a rosary during the first act but he certainly could have done with it. However, apart from that, it was a highly successful evening, and I remember we ended up taking coffee at 11.30 p.m. seated outside at a pavement cafe near the Opera House, and having a good laugh.

* * *

On another evening out at the theatre also up in "the gods", I was watching an amusing play "Off the Record" with a schoolfriend, Richard Parsons, who was a descendant of Sir Charles Parsons, the inventor of the steam turbine.

Richard was smoking, so one can tell that it was quite a long time ago, and he, like myself, had become completely engrossed by the hilariously funny play and failed to notice where the ash from his cigarette was falling. I suddenly realised that he was fidgeting and peering down on the floor beside him and then at the back of the person in front. "Look," I hastily whispered to him. The man in front of us was leaning forward in order the better to see the stage and Richard's ash was falling between his shirt and his jacket. I am embarrassed to add that our mirth was no longer for the play, but for the situation close to us.

* * *

On holiday once in Venice I attended no less than five classical concerts – Bach, Vivaldi, Beethoven, Brahms and others. It reminded me of the importance of not just having music as a background, but of really listening and giving one's whole attention to it.

* * *

On another occasion I went to a concert in Hull City Hall given by the Yorkshire Symphony Orchestra conducted by Sir Thomas Beecham. The only seats available were two shillings, (it was in 1949) in the very front row. There were two of us and we were only a few feet away from the rostrum where the great man stood. We could not only see Thomas Beecham but we could clearly hear him as well, and I recall especially during The Trojan March by Berlioz, which is a loud piece of music, he was shouting most of the time at, and with the orchestra. This wasn't so much because they weren't doing what he wanted, but because he just couldn't refrain from joining in with them. You could see this by his face. On coming forward for the fifth time to respond to the applause, he said a few words to the effect that he hoped the people of Hull realised the worth of their magnificent orchestra!

* * *

Man is a celebrating animal and celebrations are important in all our lives, and particularly when centred around the meal table, and there have been so many experiences of this in different parts of the world. They can take on varying forms as was the case once when in Norway. It was after Kristin's ordination at the end of May in the Lutheran church near Tromso.

The local Mayor and his wife had invited Kristin and her family and closest friends to a luncheon in the village hotel. John and I were included and it was a most enjoyable event. The hotel was quite an old one, with ancient wood furniture and a great log fire in the lounge, although this was hardly necessary as the day was the warmest they'd had for the whole year; the cold wind had almost completely dropped and the sun was blazing in a clear sky. I was sitting opposite Kristin's father who was Professor of Philosophy at Tromso University, and who had spent a year at Oxford with his family four years ago, and so knew England quite well.

We ate some cooked reindeer, and the dessert was the finest crème caramel I'd ever tasted. One of Kristin's cousins, who is a doctor, was sitting next to me and she remarked that it was the best she had tasted too! There was no alcohol at all at the meal, probably due to the fact that nearly everyone there was driving and the Norwegians are very strict indeed about the drink/driving rule. We could probably learn a lesson from them.

It was a really great and joyful celebration which was continued later in the evening, or I should say during the night, as well after 1 a.m. we were sitting outside Kristin's house sipping coffee in broad daylight – it being the time of the midnight sun, which hovered well above the horizon.

* * *

One day in Jamaica we sat down and ate jackfruit which was a very intriguing sort of fruit grown in the topics which I had never seen or tasted before. I had to steel myself to use my fingers to get out the soft, sweet part of it which was the edible portion but when I achieved that and overcame my sensitivities I found it quite delicious. The stones are apparently roasted and these too can be good to eat.

Less inviting is the custom of eating the whole of a fish, the eyes and most of the head, indeed everything except the very thick bone. I have not adopted this custom as it can be very easy even to get a hard cooked brittle piece of bone stuck in one's throat. I'm also not too keen on the very thought of eating the eyes! I should add that, in addition to the fish heads, I try to avoid the chicken feet and pigs' tails, both of which are frequently on the menu!

We read of Jesus frequently sharing a meal with his disciples, and this can be an excellent use of leisure time in our lives. I found whilst in Australia, that the most frequent topics of conversation were leisure activities such as travel, wildlife, food and drink. Perhaps this sums up much of how our leisure is spent. It is best if it involves positive activity rather than staring passively at the TV or computer screen. It then becomes in some part creative and therefore caught up in the creative movement of God, the Trinity.

In this pressurised age then, let us not overlook the importance of our leisure time, whether it be entertainment or activity, music or meals, travel or laughter.

⋆ ⋆ ⋆

The Truth and the Light of Love

Today many are in a similar position to that of Pilate who was puzzled by the strong condemnation of Jesus by the Jews. "What is truth?", Pilate asks. Is Jesus really the Truth and the Life, the answer to life's meaning?

Jesus frequently accused people of their blindness. He came to heal them, not only of their physical blindness, but, most important of all, their spiritual blindness. Furthermore, he said, "Let your light be seen". Light allows the truth to be seen. With those who were blind Jesus frequently caused them to see, both spiritually and physically.

Several times in the liturgy of the Mass we pray that we may keep faithful to the light of God's truth. However, like many in the crowd witnessing Jesus' trial, we too, often fail to acclaim and acknowledge him as we should. We fail in love.

⋆ ⋆ ⋆

There is an enormous twelfth century chandelier in the Cathedral at Aix-la-Chapelle with forty eight candles decorating the octagon which has representations of the eight beatitudes and eight scenes from the life of Christ. May the life, the light and the truth of Christ be seen.

The parish priest in a small village came back after seeing it and announced that he was going to install a chandelier in the church. Immediately a parish meeting was called to discuss the matter, with the result that, unanimously, the parishioners agreed that they did not want a chandelier in the church.

"First" the chairman informed the priest, "half of us can't spell it. Secondly, no one can play it, and thirdly, what we really want is a little more light!"

* * *

I have encountered many people who are blind or partially sighted. Often at the seminary in Paris I would visit Madame le Moal and write letters for her or read to her. Once I accompanied her and a coach-load of other blind people on an outing in the country. One of them wanted to stop for the toilet. We were on a long open stretch of road and there being no toilet on the coach and the need was urgent, we stopped. The person whose need was great was helped out, only to be followed by others who decided they also had a similar need. Nearly all, both men and women, ended up spread along the grass sward, relieving themselves. Madame le Moal, who could see a little, remarked to me, "Oh dear, what must you think of us?"

José Murdoch who used to be my most efficient secretary when I was in Aylesbury later suffered from failing sight and had to rely on talking books, thanks to modern technology.

And then my father, for the last 25 years of his life also made use of talking books and even taught himself to use a typewriter to type letters and to write his memoirs.

⋆ ⋆ ⋆

To follow Christ we must be honest and truthful. This frequently means not following the way of the media. The latter is often not renowned for its adherence to truth. I once preached at an Anglican Remembrance Day Service. The local press were there and to my horror they quoted something I had said completely out of context.

I had tried to show the importance of remembering the dead, praying for them and living up to the principles for which they gave their lives. As a preamble to this I had mentioned some of the good things we remember about war, as well as its horrors. This was distorted to suggest that war, for all its grim side, was part of God's plan for keeping the population in check and channelling the energies of the young!

⋆ ⋆ ⋆

There was once a man who, like Pilate, asked the question, "What is truth?" When a boy, he asked his parents, his teachers, at university and later, his colleagues at work. Basically they all told him that he'd have to get on with life and then he'd find out.

He eventually married and had a family, but he still felt that he had to find out what truth was. The years passed and finally he was advised to go to a certain place, far away, up in the mountains and there he would find a wise person who would answer his question. He climbed up as directed and there he finally came to a cave where lived a very ugly old woman. He posed his question, "Are you the truth?"

"Yes, I am," she replied.

"I've been searching for so long," he answered, "and now I've found you. When I go back, what should I tell everyone?"

"Tell them I'm very beautiful," she replied, "and that's the truth."

⋆ ⋆ ⋆

Religion should be honest and true; and this is the reason why artificial flowers are discouraged when associated with worship.

⋆ ⋆ ⋆

The Italians, however, especially in the Baroque period, seem to have gone in for the "trompe d'oeil". I noticed it in the façade of what is now the hospital next to the church of San Giovanni e Paolo in Venice as well as elsewhere. The most fantastic I think was in the church of Carmini in Florence where in the ceiling you really found it almost impossible to distinguish the real from the false.

⋆ ⋆ ⋆

A seven-year old boy asked his Dad where he came from when he was a baby. The father replied: "A stork brought you." "And you Dad, where did you come from?"to which he had the same reply, "A stork."

"And what about Grandma?" persisted the boy.

"A stork," replied the father.

The young lad wrote in his school notebook, “There’ve been no natural births in our family for three generations.” It is always important to tell children the truth.

⋆ ⋆ ⋆

A mother couldn’t do anything to stop her small child from continually sucking his thumb. Finally she said, “If you keep on sucking your thumb, you’re going to get fatter and fatter and fatter – and then, one day you’ll burst!” The youngster was terrified and stopped. Shortly afterwards he was on a bus and seated the other side of the gangway was a young lady nearly nine months pregnant. He looked across at her and in a loud voice said, “I know what you’ve been doing.”

⋆ ⋆ ⋆

I once met a “footstep artist”. There are only about twelve in the country. They make sound effects for films, documentary programmes, etc. For example, in a nature film, one might see a frog splashing into the water and then hear the splash. He explained that it was not really the splash of the frog because the photograph would have been taken with a telescopic lens and in no way would there be a microphone near enough to the frog to catch the sound it made. Hence the footstep artist is one who fabricates the sound, and he’d do it by splashing his hand into a bowl of water.

He kept several of us very entertained for the evening, explaining how various sounds were made. Footsteps through the snow, for example, would be variations on squeezing a bag of semolina, and in a murder film where somebody is stabbed or has his head cut off, he would make use of a cabbage with a knife going through it.

★ ★ ★

Cardinal Cormac Murphy-O'Connor once recounted the story of four tailors in the same street in a town in Poland. They each had a notice in their shop window. The first one had the sign "The best tailor in the town." The second tailor thought he would go one better and his notice read "The best tailor in Poland." Not to be outdone the third tailor's notice read "The best tailor in the world." Seeing the notices the other three had put up the fourth tailor wrote, "The best tailor in the street." He was nearer the truth and perhaps a reminder to some of the misleading advertisers in our media today.

★ ★ ★

"Two men came down a chimney. One is clean, the other is dirty. Which one will go to have a wash?"asked the wise man.

"The one who is dirty," replied the disciple.

"Not at all," replied the wise man, "the one who is clean. Seeing his companion dirty, he says to himself: "Since he is dirty, I must also be and so I need to go for a wash" whereas the one who is dirty, seeing his companion clean, says, "Since he is clean, then so must I be." Hence I've no need to go for a wash'."

The wise man continued – "Two men came down a chimney. One is clean the other is dirty. Which one will go for a wash?"

"The one who is clean," said the disciple, enthusiastically.

"Certainly not! The one who is dirty. Seeing his hands full of soot, he says to himself, 'I'm dirty. I must have a wash'. The other who is clean, seeing his hands clean, says 'As I'm not dirty, I've no need to wash'."

The wise man continued: -"Two men came down a chimney. One is clean the other is dirty. Which one will go for a wash?"

The disciple thought he had at last understood. "The dirty one and the clean one," he replied.

"Wrong!" said the wise man. "You haven't understood that if two men come down a chimney, it's impossible that only one is dirty whilst the other remains clean. In fact both must be dirty! When a problem is badly posed all the answers are wrong."

* * *

The truth of God's presence in our lives is frequently revealed through providential happenings, events that many today would describe as coincidences or synchronicity. For myself, I am quite sure that they are indications of the hand of God guiding us, guiding us towards the Truth.

* * *

The following is one of many similar examples that could be quoted by most priests and many lay people.

It was lunchtime during our Diocesan Assembly at the Becket school and I decided to dash back for a sandwich at Cathedral House in order to avoid the long queues at the school where the Assembly was being held. Just as I was about to return to the Assembly, the phone went. It was a sick call at the hospital. I called out to Angela, who had answered the call, "Get Father Harris or another priest to deal with it." Then I had a second thought and decided that I might just have time to call at the hospital on my way back to the Assembly. I drove down and found that it was an elderly lady, who was clearly quite ill. One of the nurses was holding her hand.

The nurse left and I proceeded to speak to the person, as although she was clearly unconscious, the hearing is very often alert at that time, and I told her that I was a priest and that I was going to give her the Sacrament of the Sick as a sign of God's loving presence with her, and to put her trust in Him. There was a slight reaction as I said this. I then proceeded to pray and to lay hands on her as part of the Sacrament. As I took my hands off her head I just noticed a very slight and weak movement, and as I was unscrewing the holy oils container I just thought that she had stopped breathing. I looked again, but was not sure, so I thought I had better continue with the Sacrament and I then anointed her and concluded with a prayer and a blessing. I then tried to find her pulse (as I was more and more convinced that she had in fact died). I went out and found the Sister who came and agreed – yes, she was dead. I praised God that I had answered the call promptly.

⋆ ⋆ ⋆

Pope Benedict in addressing the young people in Sydney made the point that our lives are not governed by chance: our very existence is willed by God and our lives are not just a succession of events or experiences, but a search for the true, the good and the beautiful – and it is in this that we find happiness and joy.

⋆ ⋆ ⋆

It was Sunday but also Jamaican Independence Day, so I began at Mass by saying it was perhaps the humour of Providence that an Englishman was saying Mass on that day. In the afternoon I went down to say a second Mass for the residents and sisters at Mother Teresa's community. There was a youngish sister, Soeur Jeanne d'Arc, there who was white skinned – most of the others were from India – and I decided she must be either European or American. In fact it turned out that she was French and her family came form Meudon which is the suburb of Paris next to the seminary where I had studied. We chatted a little and then discovered that Cardinal Feltin who had ordained me priest in Notre Dame in 1960 was a cousin of her father's and she remembered as a child sitting on his knee and undoing the red buttons on his cassock!

⋆ ⋆ ⋆

A visitor arrived in the square of a small town in Ireland. He saw two hotels, and approached a man who was leaning against a wall. "Excuse me, but could you tell me, which of those two hotels would you recommend?" "Well, sir," was the reply. "it's like this: if you chose the one, you'd wish you'd chosen the other." How does Providence come into such decisions?

⋆ ⋆ ⋆

To follow the truth we have to be enlightened by love.

The Truth and Love's Failings

Failures to love can vary in degree and kind. There can be simple misunderstandings for which no one is really to blame. They are often the result of our human condition and of poor communication and they, unfortunately, give rise to arguments and the break up of relationships. Then there is forgetfulness, which is common to us all, no matter what our age. Sometimes this is through our own failure to make an effort to remember, or write down reminders.

Pride, in its various forms, wars against love and humility, and inefficiency in the work we undertake, can easily be the cause of accidents. Hatred, violence and warfare are the worst enemies of love; and in all of our failures to love, anxiety, doubt and worry infiltrate.

* * *

Dr Charles Mayo of Mayo Clinics says 'there is a mountain of evidence to suggest worry is the chief contributor to depression, nervous breakdowns, high blood pressure, heart attacks and early death. Stress kills.'

Psychologists tell us:

30% of what we worry about never happens
30% has already happened
12% is on unfounded health concerns
20% involves worrying about trivial matters
That leaves 8%!
We worry 92% of the time for no good reason at all!

* * *

The great good news is that all our failures to love can be forgiven and healed through the Sacrament of Reconciliation infused with a genuine spirit of repentance.

* * *

The following are a few random examples of misunderstandings.

At the beginning of World War II, I was 9 years old and had heard that we were to be issued with gas-masks. However, I thought they were something to do with the cooking. Imagine, then, my amazement and fright when one evening the local carpenter-cum-undertaker arrived with gas masks for us all and thrust one over my face: it was such a horribly smelly thing, and I ran out of the room frantically pulling it off.

* * *

A well-known example is a transcript of the ACTUAL radio conversation of a British Naval ship and the Irish, off the cost of Kerry, October 1995 released by the Chief of Naval operations:

IRISH: Please divert your course 15 degrees to the South, to avoid a collision.

BRITISH: Recommend you divert your course 15 degrees to the South, to avoid a collision.

IRISH: Negative. You need to divert your course 15 degrees to the South to avoid a collision.

BRITISH: This is the Captain of a British Navy ship. I say again, DIVERT your course.

IRISH: Negative. I say again, you will have to divert your course.

BRITISH: This is the Aircraft Carrier HMS Britannia. The second largest ship in the British Atlantic Fleet. We are accompanied by three destroyers, three cruisers, and numerous support vessels. I demand that you change your course 15 degrees north, or counter-measures will be undertaken to ensure the safety of this ship.

IRISH: We are a lighthouse. Your call.

* * *

Pheasants always remind me of the disaster at Aylesbury when I had insisted on cooking a meal with oven-ready pheasants to celebrate a reunion after a Holy Land pilgrimage. I had interpreted 'oven-ready' literally and had put the pheasants in the oven, wondering why there was such a pungent and indeed rather objectionable odour after about an hour or so. It permeated the whole of the presbytery. Some of the plastic bags which I had failed to remove had burst and the results were beyond one's imaginings. A quick visit to the Co-op to buy some substitute cold ham had to be made.

* * *

At school during my teens I made several efforts to exercise my somewhat mediocre musical skills. These comprised singing in the choir, playing piano duets, hymns at the morning assembly, and most memorable of all, percussion in the school orchestra. It was the last, when put on the tubular bells, that caused me to be banished from the whole musical arena.

It was during a school concert, which included Bach's Christmas Overture, and I was standing at the ready behind the set of tubular bells, the music master who was conducting having instructed me to make several 'peels' with bells going down the scale each time. He would give me a signal when to start. Unfortunately the cellists were in front of me and I mistook the sign given to them, thinking it was for me.

I started and once in full swing my whole attention was concentrated on giving an even peel and I had no regard for the conductor's frantic gestures or the subsequent clash of sound with the other instruments! I now enjoy just listening to music.

* * *

The parents of a small boy aged nine were very worried at his habit of killing birds with a catapult. They could not stop him. A friend said, "Ah, sex is the cause of this." "Nonsense" said the parents, "he's only nine years old". "Never mind," said the friends. "That's what it is. I should take him to a psychiatrist." So they did.

The psychiatrist asked him what he liked doing best of all. After much hesitation the boy said: "I like taking down little girl's pants." Ah, thought the psychiatrist, that's it,

SEX. "Why do you like taking down little girls' pants?" "Well, because then I get more elastic to make more catapults to kill more birds."

* * *

On a more serious note: tiredness and distractions can cause love to fail as seen in the following.

On one occasion when I was a curate I was awakened by the telephone at 6.55 a.m. on Christmas morning. It was the hospital 'phoning to know where the priest was to say the 6.45 Mass. I had had the usual busy Christmas Eve and Midnight Mass and had not heard my alarm.

Another occasion that stands out in my mind was at R.A.F. Cosford enjoying a Sunday lunch with some friends, and at about 4.15 p.m. just before I was about to leave, they asked me to arrange a day to go out with them. I opened my diary, turned the pages, and my eye fell on that same Sunday afternoon that I was enjoying with them at that moment, and to my horror found that I should have been doing a baptism at 3 p.m. in the church. Discovering something like that makes one feel as if one is hanging upside down and then being pulled in all directions. In this particular case I immediately 'phoned the family and found that they were all back at home, enjoying a baptismal party without having had the baptism. But it was worse, as the husband, in a rather cool voice, explained that it wouldn't have been so bad but at the baptism of their first child the priest had been very late, and for their marriage in a Catholic church, the priest had forgotten to turn up altogether.

They eventually chose to have the baptism the following week. It was one of the most embarrassing moments of my life. Baptisms, weddings and funerals are such important events, and in addition, for many non-Catholics who come it is the only contact they have with the Catholic Church.

⋆ ⋆ ⋆

I hear and I forget;
I see and I remember;
I do and I understand.

⋆ ⋆ ⋆

Perhaps the most notable examples of a failure to love are when we fail to practise humility: once when in Edinburgh a friend remarked on the number of golf courses: Mrs Mackie replied, "Ooh, you're nobody if you don't play golf"; and Mr Mackie's dour rejoinder was, "We don't play golf!"

⋆ ⋆ ⋆

Cardinal Hume once remarked that when people praise you, "Enjoy it, but don't inhale!"

⋆ ⋆ ⋆

Two mountain goats once met on a narrow plant bridge which spanned a deep ravine. They wanted to pass each other; but there was no room, and they both realised that if they were to butt or push each other, they would fall into the abyss together. The situation was a deadlock.

One goat was very proud, and would not give in; but the other was more sensible. He lay down on the plank, and let the second walk over him to the opposite side. Then he got up and went safely over too. Someone always has to begin.

⋆ ⋆ ⋆

In September 1948 I was made a prefect at school. I was quite dazed to hear this as I was no good in the world of sport and not exceptional at work, and there were others who had not been asked. My duties consisted of seeing that all boys wore school ties and caps, and did not walk with their hands in their pockets. At meal times I had to encourage them in good manners, particularly the new boys who were, on the whole, a tough lot. Just two days later I was elected Shooting Captain for Raleigh House. My highest score had been only 89%, so I felt that I'd have to improve a lot in this. I began to learn, realising my own inadequacies, the importance of not being proud.

⋆ ⋆ ⋆

At a special service at Holy Sepulchre Church, Northampton in June 1989 Prince Charles and Princess Diana were present; they passed less than an arm's length from me as I was standing on the gangway together with a number of other clergy and their wives, mostly from the town centre churches. As Prince Charles passed us he looked at us and said with a broad smile - "There are a lot of parsons here today." Wilf Diggin, the U.R.C. minister, who was next to me whispered immediately, "Do you think we could count that as having spoken to us?" I nodded and somewhat untruthfully said, "Definitely, yes."

* * *

I cannot resist including the following near-accident, which may have been due to lack of inspection. Frogmore, in the grounds of Windsor Castle is a pleasant country house, situated in well-planned gardens, and used by royalty. The tombs of Queen Victoria and Price Albert are in an impressive domed mausoleum in the grounds. Four of us joined the crowds one day, taking advantage of one of the few occasions when it was open to the public. I was just a few feet in front of the other three as we went into the mausoleum, when I suddenly heard behind me a heavy clatter of metal. I turned around thinking that one of the others had knocked over something. In fact it was a two foot metal bar which had fallen from the roof just in front of Imre and Ryta and Liz. A few inches nearer, and it would have landed on one of their heads.

It was an alarming moment. Attendants came forward, the mausoleum was immediately closed to the public and by way of compensation, we were offered four free tickets to the house. The full seriousness of the incident dawned on me later during the night, and the next morning I wrote to the Queen about it and received in reply an apologetic letter assuring me that a full inspection would be carried out!

* * *

I'm a little asthmatic and an attack can often be activated by certain perfumes. There was a certain lady – and I never discovered who she was – who every few months would come to me to confession in the Cathedral. I would be seated in my small confessional, which offered the choice of a face to face confession or through the grille. She would always go to the latter where I was unable to see her.

However I smelt her come in. She used a highly pungent, and doubtless cheap, perfume, and I was assailed by this very strong odour, which, within seconds caused me to wheeze and cough. The result was that whatever sins she may have committed and confessed were absolved in no time at all before I thankfully told her: "Go in peace." I reflected some years later that, for her penance, I should have told her to abstain from perfume!

⋆ ⋆ ⋆

Some think it is a sin to doubt. It is certainly quite normal to question and wonder and to have difficulties with regard to our faith. We sometimes go through periods of darkness and we are unable to see the light at the end of the tunnel, and that is where perseverance comes in: just hanging on. I'm sure this is something of what Our Lady must have experienced at the time of the Annunciation and even right up to the moment she stood at the foot of the cross.

⋆ ⋆ ⋆

What is the difference between "conscience" and "conscious"?

Boy: "Conscious" is when you're aware of something, and "conscience" is when you wish you weren't.

* * *

Patrick Brent, caretaker at the Middle School, several times caused fires at the school, usually subsequent to being reprimanded by the Headmaster for not cleaning the toilets properly! On the last occasion it was quite a serious fire. Staff and parents rallied around to help clear up the mess and the caretaker was there kindly making cups of tea for the volunteers. It was he, also, who had "discovered" the fire and called the fire brigade. Brent had been an air gunner during the second world war and had several medals to his credit.

Fire seemed to be the order of the day in Fordbury, as a year later, there was one at St Joseph's church. It was started by a lad who'd had a bad day at school. The psychiatrist said that he could have thrown a brick through a window, but instead he set light to a curtain in the church. There were no candles alight near the blue velvet curtains where the fire is believed to have started and less than three feet from the curtains, which were completely destroyed in the fire, stood the tabernacle which housed the Eucharist. But its fire-proof outer casing remained unscathed.

The fire could have had more serious consequences but for the prompt action of the 15 Fordbury firemen. Using breathing apparatus they prevented the fire from spreading throughout the smoke-filled church and into the living quarters, where my elderly parents, both in their eighties, were also living. The telephone was soon jammed with calls offering help, and parishioners turned up the following morning to help clean the church. An Anglican clergyman rang up to offer his church premises, a trader sent flowers to cheer everyone up and the Salvation Army sent round a little army of helpers.

We had scaffolding in the church for weeks and flowers and Mass cards were hung over the bars on the occasion of my mother's funeral several months later.

⋆ ⋆ ⋆

When I think back over my life I suppose I've oscillated regarding the pros and cons of pacifism. When at university it was a burning question, and then I found that the Catholic Church advocated certain reasons to justify warfare. In a certain sense I accepted them, although I remember arguing in some ways against them from time to time.

Then when I was on the O.C.T.U. preparing to be commissioned in the R.A.F. for my National Service, I was horrified at some of the things we learnt, but my inner convictions were very much shelved – and shelved again when I went into the R.A.F. as a chaplain, although it was there in the background and certainly came to the fore when I was asked if I would like to sign on for sixteen years. I felt the answer to that must certainly be 'NO'. As a chaplain one's primary care was with human beings who happened to be trained for warfare, and they had souls to be saved, but I still felt that to be so committed to wearing a uniform, and with a rank, would be going against my convictions. And so I, with the bishop's agreement, opted out of the Services.

Now, increasingly, I've reflected on the whole question of war and on those words of Our Lord, "You have learned how it is said eye for eye and tooth for tooth but I say this to you – offer the wicked man no resistance", and then Our Lord goes on to talk about, and expound on the law of love. "Offering the wicked man no resistance", means that wickedness will infiltrate into our world, into our lives, but we must not oppose it with further wickedness but offer him the other cheek as well.

And then it struck me very forcibly on reading Paul's words in the beginning of his Letter to the Corinthians where he says that the language of the Cross may be illogical to those who are not on the way to salvation, but those who are on the way see it as God's power to save. Christ Himself did not offer resistance but allowed Himself to be crucified, and it is in that allowing of the evil to happen without opposing it by further evil and violence, that ultimate good reigns, and this in the eyes of the world is utter folly. Many have not grasped this message, but the Church is now coming round much more to a pacifist view, especially with regard to weapons of mass destruction.

* * *

And then lastly, we come to the more obvious of love's failings- hatred, force and violence.

During World War II there was the story that Hitler, Mussolini and Churchill met for a secret conference. Hitler wanted Churchill to sign up admitting defeat. Churchill wouldn't but suggested that the first one to catch the carp swimming in a nearby pool without using any fishing equipment would be the winner. The others agreed. Hitler took out a revolver to shoot the fish, but each shot was deflected by the water. Mussolini jumped into the pool but failed to catch the carp with his hands. Churchill took out a spoon, dipped it many times into the water, throwing the water over his shoulder. "It will take a long time," said Churchill, "But we are going to win the war."

⋆ ⋆ ⋆

An inspiring piece of writing is John Pridmore's story of his conversion "From Gangland to Promised Land" (2002).

The author of this outstanding piece of autobiographical writing compliments the publishers for being adventurous enough to commission the book. This is understandable, for it is not in the style of the usual story of a person's progress – from cabin boy to Admiral, or from errand lad to Prime Minister.

John Pridmore's story is more like that of St Paul, except that John did not fall off a horse, but when in his mid-thirties (he is now turned 40 years old) he sat in his flat in the early hours of the morning and heard the Lord recounting the worst things he had ever done and the evils he had perpetuated: theft, violence, near-murder, drug-pushing, working as a vicious bouncer, sex and many minor crimes, vividly described in the book, he realized that it was the voice of his conscience. He felt as if he were dying and going to hell. He cried out, "Give me another chance!" And at that moment he knew – really knew, not just believed – that God was real.

One of the first people he told about his conversion was his mother whom he found had never ceased to pray for him each day. "About two weeks ago," she told him, "I felt my prayers weren't being answered. I prayed to Jesus to take you. If it meant you dying, then to let you die, but not to let you hurt yourself or anyone else any more." The Lord always answers our prayers, but in his way and in his good time.

John describes his earlier life, as well as his struggles since, to live up to his conversion experience, in a vivid and readable book.

With the help of Greg Watts, a freelance writer, we have a story of God's grace at work: an inspiration to all, an encouragement to parents and, hopefully, a help to young people. John at present gives his energies doing retreat work for Youth 2000, and young people in general.

⋆ ⋆ ⋆

In May 2008 the media, including the tabloids, recounted the senseless stabbing of a sixteen year old lad, Jimmy Mizen one lunchtime during when he had gone to a local bakery in south east London. He was a pupil at St Thomas More Catholic Comprehensive School, quiet and well-liked and from a loving Catholic family. A reporter asked his mother if she was angry. "No," she replied, "there's quite enough anger in the world – it was anger which killed my son. If I'm angry then I'm going to be doing just exactly the same as the chap who killed my son. We've got to get rid of all this anger that is around." She then added that she felt sorry for the parents of the young man who had murdered Jimmy. "What happened to Jimmy is the worst thing possible, but we've got such wonderful memories. They haven't got wonderful memories of their son. All they can think about is the evil he's done. My prayers are with that family." The Mizens said that it was their strong faith that sustained them and inspired their attitude of forgiveness.

⋆ ⋆ ⋆

If the other person is 99% wrong and I am only 1% wrong it is easier for me to begin to change and apologise for my 1% than for my 'enemy' to begin with his 99%.

⋆ ⋆ ⋆

When William Gladstone was Chancellor of the Exchequer he asked the statistician in the Treasury to give him certain figures on which to base his forthcoming speech in the Commons. The figures he'd been given were incorrect and Gladstone was publicly ridiculed. Gladstone sent for the man responsible and instead of chastising him, told him that he understood how fearful and embarrassed he must be, praised him for his good work in the past and expressed his appreciation and forgiveness for the mistake.

⋆ ⋆ ⋆

A driver stalled her car. She kept trying to start it again but with no success. There were angry hoots from the man in the car behind. Finally the lady got out and went to him: "Shall we change places?" she said, "You try starting my car and I'll honk on your horn?"

⋆ ⋆ ⋆

There was a big chestnut tree in the Cathedral House garden and every year in the autumn children used to invade the garden and throw up sticks to try and knock down the conkers. I told them not to, and one day Lucy got hurt: one of the sticks had fallen and hit her, breaking her glasses, cutting her face and she had to go to hospital. The children kept away for the next ten days. It then rained and the conkers fell naturally. There was no need to knock them down. Patience – and they fell in their own time. It is like that with us.

* * *

Father Gordon Albion, who received me into the Church, used to say that there are two things bad for the heart: running upstairs and running down people.

* * *

On one occasion Pope John-Paul II prayed in public for pardon: for the divisions amongst Christians; for the violence which some of them used in the service of the truth; and for the attitudes of diffidence and hostility adopted towards followers of other religions.

Christians should also confess their share of responsibility "for the evils of today"; for atheism, religious indifference, secularism, ethical relativism, violations of the right to life, lack of interest in the poverty of many countries.

At the same time, the Pope said, "Let us forgive the wrongs done by others to us."

* * *

At the entrance to the Church of Reconciliation at Taizé, which was built by Germans as an act of reparation for the atrocities of World War II, is the inscription:

"Be reconciled all you who enter here:
Parents and children,
Husbands and wives,
Believers and those who cannot believe,
Christians and their fellow Christians."

* * *

The Life and its Guidelines

To follow the way of Jesus, the way of love, and to love his life, a shared life, we need certain pointers, guidelines. The law of love needs to be spelt out in some detail.

A few guidelines of the Catholic Church on some of the current moral issues may be helpful

The Catholic Christian faith is all about love and life, based on Jesus' teaching and his claim: "I am the Way, the Truth and the Life." It may also be summed up positively in the Golden Rule: "Do to others as you would have them do to you."

This means that the human being is to be respected and treated as a person from the moment of conception – the human embryo is "not a potential human being but a human being with potential" – and this means from before implantation to the moment of death (ie. the complete and irreversible cessation of all brain activity). This, of course, rules out direct killing in both abortion and euthanasia. It also excludes in vitro fertilisation (IVF), which involves the destruction of many human embryos and it is often used for scientific experimentation. So-called therapeutic cloning of human embryos and, even worse, hybrid human and animal embryos, should not be used as a source of stem cells for medical research. Stem cells taken directly from adults are the best way forward.

Between these two moments of conception and death, the human being grows and develops and is guided along the way by certain moral principles based on love, a love that can take many forms. It can be between child and parent, members of a family, and friends. It can apply in different forms for single, celibate, as well as married people. For the last only, it includes sexual union and a union “till death do us part”.

This respect for human life and the law of love which this involves, also excludes the use of force, except as a last resort to preserve the common good or to defend ones life, for example in the case of organised crime or aggression due to drugs and drink. However, it is unlawful to use more than necessary force to preserve life.

Respect for life should stop us using capital punishment and warfare which takes the form of an act of aggression, or fails to discriminate between combatant and non-combatant, or makes use of weapons of mass-destruction. The principle of Hammurabi (an eye for an eye, a tooth for a tooth, or the rule of tit-for-tat – you hit me then I can hit you) must, according to Jesus, be surpassed by that of forgiveness and not of vengeance, and even in the case of the onslaught of terrorism, the response must be based on justice and law – and negotiation.

Love of our neighbour should involve much of the money used for armaments, the arms race and warfare, being spent on relieving poverty throughout the world, instead. Furthermore, for each human being. life, to have it to the full, should involve both time for work and time for leisure, a right care of the body (health, diet, and exercise) and the soul (time for prayer and appreciation of creation.)

⋆ ⋆ ⋆

There are times when guidelines may, perhaps, be disobeyed, as shown in this light-hearted story which comes from Australia:

After getting all the Pope's luggage loaded into the limo, the driver notices that the Pope is still standing on the curb.

"Excuse me, Your Holiness," says the driver. "Would you please take your seat so we can leave?"

"Well, to tell the truth," says the Pope, "they never let me drive at the Vatican, and I'd really like to drive today."

"I'm sorry but I cannot let you do that. I'd lose my job! What if something should happen?" protests the driver, wishing he'd never gone to work that morning.

"There might be something extra in it for you," says the Pope.

Reluctantly, the driver gets in the back as the Pope climbs in behind the wheel. The driver quickly regrets his decision when, after leaving the airport, the Pontiff floors it, accelerating the limo to 105 mph.

"Please slow down, Your Holiness!!!" pleads the worried driver, but the Pope keeps the pedal to the metal until they hear sirens. "Oh, my God, I'm gonna lose my license," moans the driver.

The Pope pulls over and rolls down the window as the cop approaches, but the cop takes one look at him, goes back to his motorcycle, and gets on the radio. "I need to talk to the Chief," he says to the dispatcher.

The Chief gets on the radio and the cop tells him that he's stopped a limo going a hundred and five. "So bust him," said the Chief.

"I don't think we want to do that, he's really important," said the cop.

The Chief then asked "Who you got there, the Mayor?"

Cop: "Bigger."

Chief: "Governor?"

Cop: "Bigger."

"Well," said the Chief, "Who is it?"

Cop: "I think it's God!"

Chief: "What makes you think that?"

Cop: " He's got the Pope for a driver."

* * *

Guidelines in the form of laws and rules can sometimes by excessive and exaggerated. At the RAF OCTU course at Spitalgate there were many, that I considered to be silly, rules and regulations to obey; in fact, so many that it was difficult to remember them all. Each of us was allotted 1000 points, 500 of these were for officer qualities and 500 for knowledge of the RAF – its history, law, regulations, etc

If one was a second late for anything, points were deduced from the "officer qualities" quota, whilst failure to answer any questions on the written test papers would lose more points. A cadet ending the course with less than 600 points would not qualify as an officer. Even when off-duty, visiting the nearby town of Grantham, one was being observed and if not behaving as a potential officer, points would be lost.

One cadet, a good Catholic, happened to say to his Course Commander that if he was ordered to do something that he considered to be morally wrong, then he would refuse to do it. He was merely expressing his freedom of conscience, however, this was something the Forces would not allow. The person concerned was hauled up before the Group Captain and because he still refused to give in and agree to obey orders, even if they went against his conscience, he was expelled from the course.

* * *

Rules can also be overdone, as in the case of the instructions for access to a flat where I once stayed in Venice:

"All occupiers of this flat should note that there is a 10" tall metal flood barrier running across the floor in the lift-landing on the ground floor. Please take great care not to stumble over it, and warn all members of your party.

The lift itself is on your left as you enter the downstairs hall. On arrival please comply with the regulations: max. weight = 3 large people. Always close all five doors of the lift. Press the control buttons slowly and well in, to avoid jamming. Call the lift by pressing the call-button on the wall. If red light displays "Occupato" (= engaged), either someone is using the lift, or one of the doors has been left open at one of the upper floors. In this case do not lose patience but climb upstairs (3rd or 4th floor) and fetch the cabin down to the ground-floor. Press T for ground floor. Four people with luggage require only three trips in the lift. Once you are all out on the third floor landing, close carefully by hand the five doors of the lift and watch the red light on the call-button by the lift go off. If it does not go off, then one of the doors has not been properly closed. Please check them all again. As a matter of precaution, when in a hurry, it is wise to use the stairs to avoid any possible delay due to unforeseeable lift breakdown. Furthermore, it is advisable that a party should not go all together in the lift, but should split company, so that one person is always out of the lift, ready to come to the rescue should the cabin stop between floors, trapping people inside. Failure to heed this warning could result in a whole party being trapped in the lift for days, as the alarm bell cannot be heard outside the building."

After reading this we felt it advisable to avoid using the lift on any occasion.

⋆ ⋆ ⋆

Some laws and rules can and do frequently change. For example from 1300 to 1500 it was illegal for Englishmen to eat three meals a day, and in the reign of Queen Elizabeth the first men with beards had to pay a levy!

⋆ ⋆ ⋆

A nun was once recounting the old times before many of the Church rules changed. It was shortly before Easter and this particular Sister was preparing a simnel cake. She was stirring it and inadvertently put a raisin in her mouth. Mass was to follow and it meant she had broken her fast so she told this tragic happening to the Mother Superior who was immediately in a flutter. She said "We'll have to see Father about it." It would have been so embarrassing for this poor nun to have remained in her seat while the other Sisters went up in lines to communion.

So Reverend Mother went to Father just before he was coming out for the Mass: "Father, a terrible thing has happened. I wonder if I could have a dispensation for one of the Sisters – she swallowed a raisin just a short time ago while she was cooking," to which the priest replied, very seriously "My God she might as well have swallowed a pork chop!"

★ ★ ★

A taxi driver in Rome was conveying a visitor to his destination and kept going over all the red lights. He explained to his customer: "For an Italian, the lights are a statement; to a Frenchman, an invitation; to an Englishman, a command."

★ ★ ★

Someone I know wrote to me before he stopped practising as a Catholic. His reasons, he explained, were the inhuman rules of the Church regarding contraception and homosexuality, restrictive dogmas, coupled with liberal pastoral interpretations, and a lack of silence in a wordy liturgy.

★ ★ ★

There are different sorts of guidelines, some very important and others less so. Maybe they can be categorised rather like the differing purposes proclaimed when a bell is sounded. Bells sound in different ways for different purposes: there is the alarm bell, the school bell, door bell, telephone bell, fire alarm bell, a leper's bell, cow bell, consecration bell, church bell, sleigh bells, and monastery bells.... and they are all calling to us differently.

It think I was near Cong in Ireland that I visited the remains of an abbey and was intrigued to be told that attached to the abbey there had been a fishing house inside which there was a fish trap which rang a bell in the monastery kitchen whenever a fish was trapped in it.

* * *

Jesus gave us the guidelines we need in seed-form and the role of the Church is to see how they apply to our lives in today's world.

* * *

There are times when the guidelines don't seem to work or when we lack the patience to allow them to. I am reminded of the case of a friend who was queuing up for a lottery ticket. It was in Ireland where one could never queue anywhere without speaking to those around one. In this case my friend turned to the lady in front of her and asked, "Have you ever won anything?"

"No," was the reply, "I'm always like someone who's given a fork to eat their soup."

There are times when our conscience must guide us to make use of a spoon!

* * *

The Life and Compassion

I have always been struck by the fact that the last story Jesus told (Matthew $25_{31\text{-}49}$) was about showing love and compassion to all who are in need, and his last action on the occasion of the celebration of the Eucharist, was that of humble service as he washed the feet of his disciples.

In the story of the Good Samaritan, the priest and the Levite may have thought: If I stop to help this man, what will happen to <u>me</u>?" The Samaritan reversed the question: "If I do not stop to help this man, what will happen to <u>him</u>?"

* * *

There have been many occasions when I have taken part in a broadcast on the radio and they have seldom caused me to be particularly nervous, but when it came to appearing on television, well, that was another matter! On the one occasion when I did take part in a televised programme, I became so worked up that I decided it was not my 'forte'.

However, I recently found the script of that one occasion and I insert it here as it relates to the Good Samaritan story.

Epilogue for Anglia TV.

Good evening. I'm sure if you suddenly heard the screech of brakes, the crunching sound of metal against metal in the road outside, you'd immediately abandon this television screen and rush out to see what had happened, and in what way you could help – caring for anyone who was injured, phoning, if you're on the phone, for the ambulance and the police, and so on........

Regardless of whom you found outside, whether he came from China or Africa, whether he turned out to be a Hindu, or a Catholic, no matter who it was, you wouldn't hesitate to help.

You would, in fact be acting very much like the Samaritan in the story Christ once told, the Samaritan who helped someone who turned out to be his arch enemy, the Orthodox Jew. Most of us these days, if we're called upon in similar circumstances would behave pretty well as the good Samaritan did, wouldn't we? And it's fairly safe to say that we would, because it's probably very seldom that we encounter an accident and someone needing help. BUT, have you thought of all the people around you who have what one might call "slow accidents"? – those who have the accident of gradually turning in on themselves and becoming lonely; those who slowly drift from experimenting with mild drugs to going on to the hard stuff; those who drop out; those who contract an incurable disease; young people who just haven't grown up, perhaps through no fault of their own............... You see there are accidents happening to people all around us all the time, not chaps being knocked off donkeys and being robbed and left half dead, not with the alarming sound of metal smashing against metal, but much more slowly and gradually and easily overlooked. And we have to try to help in these situations as well............Goodnight and God Bless you.

★ ★ ★

A top surgeon in a large city hospital always spent a few moments alone in prayer before an operation. When asked – "Yes, I always ask God to help and guide me, and especially when I'm not quite sure what next to do."

One of the greatest moments in performing any sort of work is the time given to prayer which energises us and helps us.

★ ★ ★

The great pianist Paderewski was giving a concert and the mother of a small boy took her young son, who was interested in the piano, to the concert. Whilst waiting for the concert to begin she chatted to a friend next to her. Then the lights dimmed and she suddenly realised that her son had left his seat. She glanced towards the stage and, to her amazement, saw him seated at the grand piano and starting to play "Twinkle, twinkle, little star." She was about to leap up when the great Paderewski appeared. He advanced to the keyboard. "Don't stop," he was heard to say. "Keep playing," and he reached down and began playing the bass parts with his left hand and then, encircling the youngster, he played the obligato with his right hand. God does just that with our work, no matter how insignificant it might be.

* * *

A Christian Passover Supper is a blend of the spiritual, the educational and the social. On one occasion, in Aylesbury, towards the end of the meal, at the fourth ceremonial pouring of the wine I, as father of the family, had to pour out an extra glass for Elijah. Elijah's place was always kept empty as the Jews still await his return. One of the participants on this occasion was deputed to open the door for Elijah to come in. Denis Spiller had been appointed this task and at the appropriate moment he got up, went to the door and there, just about to enter, was Jimmy.

Jimmy was a man of about 50 years of age, unemployed, homeless and with a drink problem. We had promoted him from using the dossers' hut in the garden to a bed in the parish hall. When sober, he did odd jobs about the Church and presbytery. However, on this occasion he had been on the bottle, and when Denis opened the door, Jimmy lurched in and immediately sat down at the empty place and consumed the glass of wine set there!

I later discovered that most people at the supper thought that it had all been pre-arranged and that the staging and timing of Jimmy's entrance was just perfect.

* * *

In 1980 in Kingston, Jamaica poverty and homelessness were on the increase. A Catholic priest, Father Richard Ho Lung, and several others decided that something had to be done to help those who were suffering.

People around them became aware of the problems and they were given a disused school building where they began to care for those who were homeless and often disabled, physically and/or mentally. This was just the beginning of what has now become a recognised religious congregation of men, numbering over 400, who look after the poorest of the poor. These brothers, the Missionaries of the Poor, come from different countries and their average age is about 26 years, an encouragement to those who think that youth has abandoned the Church.

Centres have been started in India, Haiti, Uganda, Kenya, the Philippines, and in Jamaica alone, some 500 people who would be otherwise homeless or dead, are given lifelong shelter and food, whilst up to a thousand others are given food each day. The money for this comes from support groups in various parts of the world, local benefactors, as well as from the proceeds from Fr. Richard's music – he is a very gifted composer of many religious songs and full-length musicals.

Volunteer workers are always welcome, and I myself have had the privilege several times of helping in the work in the centres in Kingston. There are always new experiences, for example helping with the ever increasing number of residents with AIDS in one of the centres. Most of these, who are married, have been rejected by the rest of their families. On the first day I was asked to help one of the young Brothers caring for those in the terminal stages of AIDS, who were too weak to wash themselves and had lost control of their bodily functions. This was something for which my life as a celibate priest had not prepared me. Amidst all the very basic caring jobs that had to be done each day, some would turn to me and ask fundamental questions of faith – "What is the meaning of life? What is the next life going to be like? Does God really love me? Father, what's the meaning of this line in the Gospel or Psalm?" It was a whole ministry – physical – caring for their material needs; emotional – some just wanted to share their miseries and worries as well as their joys, because Jamaicans are essentially a joyful people; and spiritual – their wish to hear one praying for them and with them.

To help in this great work in the various countries where there are Missionaries of the Poor, we have formed a charity (Missionaries of the Poor Supporters Association – MoPSA – registered charity no. 1048926) through which we send money to them regularly and we guarantee that every penny – or pound – donated goes to this great work for the poor. All administrative costs are paid for separately by various donors.

I found during my various visits to Kingston, Jamaica many opportunities and challenges to show compassion and concern for those far less fortunate than myself. Some of these are recounted in a previous book, "Shades of Welcome" and also in a fictional context, in "Central Line to Eziat". For someone who is by nature somewhat fastidious, I found many of the basic tasks of human care very unpleasant and difficult to accomplish with the necessary solicitude.

There was one blind and disabled old lady who, after I had given her lunch, indicated that she wanted to be wheeled in her chair to the toilet. I helped her out of the wheelchair – which had no workable brakes – on to the toilet and discreetly left her for a few minutes. When I returned and she indicated that she was ready to get back into the chair, I wasn't sure whether it was necessary to wipe her bottom as I did not see any paper anywhere. Then, to my horror, I found her levering herself up on one side and wiping herself with her left hand.

Later, I realised that years ago before paper was used, such tasks were always performed with the left hand, keeping your right hand for eating food and greeting one another.

⋆ ⋆ ⋆

Whilst in the centres in Jamaica there is plenty of practical help needed; perhaps an even greater need is for affection and interest, as most of the residents have been deprived of this in their infancy as well as later in life. There were quite a number whose date of birth was unknown and a few with no surnames. These were all people who had been picked up from the street and whose mental disturbance prevented them from knowing their name or when they were born.

⋆ ⋆ ⋆

In a Cheshire Home where I used occasionally to spend a few hours helping, I met John Shepherd who was paralysed from the neck down. He told me that whilst in the army he had returned to the barrack room after special duties, stood on his bunk to place a book in his locker and had slipped and fallen, breaking his neck. He recounted how he had lived through a range of emotions, complete turmoil, anger, hatred, depression, exasperation........until someone suggested that he might try drawing – with a pencil held between his teeth.

He started, and found that he had a gift for it. Painting followed until he became a skilled artist specialising in landscapes, portraits and animals.

★ ★ ★

Marie-Christine, a lively young lady from France, came to spend most of a year in the presbytery in Aylesbury while she was searching for her vocation in life. Whilst at Aylesbury, she took a temporary job as a chamber-maid in a hotel, recounting, amongst other things, that she was amazed at the waste, for example, of small pieces of soap which, used once, were thrown away. I suggested that she should bring them home for our use.

I wasn't sure that she was called to be a religious. She spent most of the next year at the Grail in Pinner to deepen the search for her vocation. However, a year following her return to France I was amazed to learn that she had joined a Carmelite Community, an enclosed order and one of the strictest, at Avranchers in the west of Normandy. "That will last at the most six months," I thought. How wrong I was. Several years later I was invited to her solemn profession and there I witnessed someone who was clearly radiantly happy, having really found her "niche" in life, responding to God's mysterious call.

We corresponded each year and I learned that her family, mother, two brothers and a sister were very opposed to her vocation and still failed to either appreciate or understand it. Then, after she had been over twenty years in the convent, I received the following letter from her, extracts of which follow.

"On the 4th December 2006 I had an accident! I fell from a ladder 4 metres high whilst working in the convent garden with the result that the pelvis and both legs were paralysed, a vertebra being broken and having compressed the spinal chord. After six months of rehabilitation I was able to return to the convent in a wheelchair, but the Lord has given me such strength and a profound joy to cope with this trial. I have been surrounded and supported by the community who have shared in my trials and I have been able to take up, once again, my life in the community being in charge, with other sisters, of the accueil (the welcome) and book-binding. The strength and the joy of the Lord is continually with me and I praise Him for His great love for me. This new stage in my life seems quite normal and I am so happy that Jesus alone can work such a miracle."

Some months later I visited her at Avranches and, whilst shocked at seeing her in a wheelchair, I was nevertheless inspired, encouraged and stimulated by the faith, the love and the joy that flowed from Sister Marie-Christ. She is an example to us all of living fully in the Way of the Lord.

This seemed to me to be a wonderful example of treating a personal tragedy positively and with great faith and courage.

⋆ ⋆ ⋆

Helen Passant from Oxford gave a talk in Northampton on healing and allied subjects. She had been a clinical nurse specialist at the Churchill hospital and had discovered how massage with various ointments for many patients who were senile had caused them to respond and react to their situation. She also spoke of the value of sound and music in therapy, and recounted the example of a man who was nearing death, and who had been visited by someone who had sat with him in silence, holding his hand for a while.

The following day the patient indicated that he didn't want this particular visitor because, he said, "she talks too much." The person in question denied having talked at all, but Helen, in probing a little further, found that she'd been sitting by the bed and saying to herself, mentally, "Oh, this is just like my father before he died", and she had gone on dreaming about her relationship with her father and all sorts of things that had happened in her childhood and her mind had been full of these matters. Helen maintained that the patient had picked this up. When a person is near to death they are more aware of what is going on around them and Helen was quite certain that a dying person can pick up vibrations and thoughts even of people around them. What then, should one do when sitting with an apparently unconscious person? Helen's reply wasm – quite simply - pray, and in the case of a non-Christian, recite a simple mantra: peace, joy, love, peace, joy, love.............

Helen herself died quite suddenly of a stroke in May 2005.

* * *

There is a power to heal through a look, a touch, a gesture, a smile, through picking up the telephone, sending an e-mail, an apology, or the spoken word.

* * *

There are moments in life when one experiences a sinking unreal sensation as if one is living in a fantasy world, a place apart from real life. This was something of what I felt when told that the result of a blood test revealed that I had cancer in the prostate and it was aggressive.

Biopsies and scans showed that it had not spread to other parts of my anatomy, but would involve a course of radio-therapy.

After the shock that inevitably the word "cancer" causes, I thought that if my life on this earth was to come to an end quite soon, then there were a few things I would like to do before that happened – one was to grow more in my faith and love and devotion to the Lord, and the other, on a more mundane level, was to re-visit Venice! The second of these I was able to put into effect some months later while the first turned out to be a slow process, which is still going on.

One day at Mount Vernon Hospital, several of us were (on one occasion) waiting in one of the rooms preparing for our daily dose of radio-therapy when an elderly man with a strong cockney accent came in, having just completed his first treatment for prostate cancer, and exclaimed: "I was in there," pointing to the inner room guarded with one foot thick protective doors, "and there were two lovely young nurses," he continued, "and one of them said 'Now take your trousers off', and the other added 'Pull your pants down.' ....what a place!"

In such situations one is certainly back to basics. I found it comical as nearly all of us men had to drink four beakers of cold water in the ten minutes before going in for the treatment; and if one failed to gauge the timing of this, one could be in trouble!

⋆ ⋆ ⋆

Richard Carr-Gomm is a remarkable man, originally an officer in the Grenadier Guards. After retiring from the guards he experienced a growing need to help lonely people. With this in mind he applied for a job as home help in Bermondsey where he performed many mundane tasks for people, mostly elderly, living alone. This led to the formation of the Abbeyfield Society, and then several years later he started up what came to be known as the Carr-Gomm Society – homes for single lonely people of all ages, with a housekeeper in charge of each home.

I was instrumental in inaugurating such a house in Aylesbury. It was an eight-roomed dwelling with a small flat for the housekeeper. Within a few weeks it was full. Initially we had various teething problems, one of which was that of following Richard Carr-Gomm's guidelines of incorporating the spiritual dimension in the running of the house. It was not to be just another boarding-house. There were to be regular, though voluntary gatherings of the residents with the housekeeper for meetings and for prayer. Happily we slowly moved into this, and the whole concept fulfilled a pressing need.

* * *

Michael Mulligan was a short stocky Irishman who had tried his vocation but had not made the grade. However, throughout his life he had wanted to help others. He used to help as cook in Bishop's House in Northampton and it was through this that he met dossers who came to the door. He would give them some soup and something to eat. This he found took time, so someone else took over the cooking and Michael, in addition to odd jobs, started running a sort of soup kitchen from the Bishop's Kitchen. As the clientele increased, he transferred it to St Patrick's Hall which stood near the front of Cathedral House. However, there was a problem, as one of the assistant priests was running a very successful youth club there. Finally, the difficultly was solved by Michael making use of the Night Shelter situated nearer the town centre. After a while Michael became dissatisfied with the running of the night-shelter, and as a result, abandoned his work with both it and the soup kitchen.

It was at this point that Valerie Hanson came on the scene. Valerie had been an actress, married with one daughter. Her husband left her, married again, and went to live in France. Valerie's daughter in the early 1980's was tragically killed in a car crash and Valerie, too, had been in an accident which had scarred her face and spoilt any chance of carrying on with her profession. She then went into teaching at RADA. Subsequent to this, in her late 50s, she became involved in helping in the soup kitchen and when Michael backed down, Valerie took over, together with nearly forty voluntary helpers, and for a number of years was of tremendous help to many of the deprived folk who frequented the kitchen.

At one point in 1988 I took her to meet Richard Carr-Gomm in Bath to discuss the possibility of opening a house for homeless youngsters. Richard and Valerie's visions differed slightly, but each listened to the other, and the project began to take shape.

* * *

The two worst illnesses in the Western World are loneliness and worry; and the two worst illnesses in the Third World are poverty and lack of food and water.

* * *

Everyday in Sister Katey's cottage in Palmas, Brazil the door – and window – was open from 7 a.m. until nearly midnight with the result that anyone and everyone would walk and in and interrupt whatever was going on, helping themselves to fruit juice or cold water from the fridge. Such was the recognised custom in that culture.

* * *

A man got into a bus and found himself sitting next to a youngster who was obviously a hippy. He was wearing only one shoe. "You've evidently lost a shoe, son". "No man," came the reply. "I found one."

* * *

Thor Heyerdahl in one of his books relates how immediately after his marriage, he and his wife spent a year on the tiny Polynesian island of Fatu-Hiva. They built their own hut and survived on the food growing on the island. They found that the local way of life excluded idleness and boredom, there was no rush and no waste, and the people were only loosely attached to personal property.

I found a similar attitude in some of the poorest of the poor whom I encountered on my visit to Kingston, Jamaica. Perhaps there is a lesson here for us all. Have we become to used to luxuries? PB, SV, HB, and Bal. (Private Bath, Sea View, Half-Board and Balcony)

* * *

Compassion and concern for others can also be shown through our generosity with whatever money we may have.

Unfortunately, money is like salt water: the more you drink, the thirstier you become.

The richest man in the world is reputed to be the Sultan of Brunei. His palace, some years ago, cost him £300,000,000 to build with a floor area large enough to build 2,500 houses. He gave a birthday party for his 11-year old daughter and arranged it at a London hotel at a cost of £200,000. My guess is that this did not make for real happiness.

In contrast is that of a very quiet unassuming man whom you'd almost pass by without noticing and who, one day, accompanied with a beautiful smile gave me a small brown envelope, saying to me quietly, "Give that to the poor people you're going to see in Jamaica."

Later, when I opened the envelope I found, in notes, £1000.00!

* * *

A very poor young artist was visiting a friend's studio and found him in the middle of painting a picture of a beggar who was seated in front of him. The beggar looked really wretched and so the young artist, although he himself was extremely poor, placed a few coins in the beggar's pocket. However, he didn't know that the beggar was really Baron Rothschild who had agreed to sit as a model for his friend as he had just the right kind of face! When the poor young artist had left, Rothschild was told that he was a gifted art student, but so poor that he was unable to complete his studies. The next day the young artist received a letter and a cheque from Baron Rothschild: "Sir," he had written, "all good deeds bear fruit sooner or later. Yesterday you gave a beggar six sous. Today those six sous have become 10,000 francs. If you will present the enclosed cheque at my banking house, you will be paid the above amount."

* * *

A man came to the door of Cathedral House looking for accommodation. I suggested he went to the Night Shelter. "Thank you, Father," he replied and then added, "You don't think you could give me two shillings, do you Father?" To which I replied, "Well, no, because shillings don't exist any more, do they?" He replied, "No, Father. I don't know what the country is coming to, do you?"

* * *

For some time I have been concerned about the peripheral adornments so frequently today attached to the celebration of the sacraments in the Church. By 'peripheral adornments' I mean customs that have developed in recent years concerning photography, parties, presents, clothes and coffins. Harvey Cox has rightly said that "man is a celebrating animal"; and it is certainly good, and indeed essential to celebrate, but we need to think carefully, and keep in proportion, what we spend on non-essentials.

* * *

Our generosity, our giving, should be like a four-pronged fork: the needs of one's family and friends; the group or church to which one belongs, those in need locally, and the needs of those in other parts of our world.

★ ★ ★

There is a story of a woman who had been used to every luxury and to great respect. She died, and when she arrived in heaven, an angel was sent to conduct her to her house. They passed many a lovely mansion and the woman thought that each one, as they came to it, must be the one allotted to her. When they had passed through the main streets they came to the outskirts, where the houses were much smaller; and on the very fringe they came to a house that was little more than a hut. "That is your house," said the conducting angel. "What," said the woman, "that! I cannot live in that." "I am sorry," said the angel, "but that is all we could build for you with the materials that you sent up."

★ ★ ★

The ideal of many today is health, wealth and prosperity and the consequent avoidance of the cross.

★ ★ ★

Charles Lamb, the writer, instead of marrying a girl whom he loved, spent 38 years looking after his mentally ill sister who had stabbed their mother to death. Such was his purpose in life and his cross.

★ ★ ★

One of my top three favourite books is "The Snow Goose" by Paul Gallico in which a disabled man uses his tiny boat to save the lives of some of the men stranded on the Dunkirk beaches in World War II. In doing this, going to and fro many times across the Channel, he himself finally lost his life.

⋆ ⋆ ⋆

All this may be summed up in C.S. Lewis's sentence, "Pain is God's megaphone to arouse a deaf world," and the Arab proverb, "Too much sunshine makes a desert."

The Life and Community

The most basic and important of human communities is, of course, the family, or at least the married couple. However, before being sufficiently mature to relate to another in marriage, or to others in a community, one must have grown in self-knowledge and awareness.

* * *

Bishop Leo used to recount the story of visiting an old people's home and going up to speak with a group who were seated in the corner of the lounge. "Do you know who I am?" he asked them by way of starting a conversation. "No," replied one lady, "but you'd better go and ask at the Reception."

There is also the story of how the same bishop was visiting a class in a junior school not long after the Pope had visited Coventry and celebrated Mass on the airfield. All the children had been at Coventry on that momentous day, and so the bishop asked them what they remembered most about the day. There was complete silence. He asked them again. Silence. He then asked if there was anything at all that they remembered about the day. Still no answer until, finally, one child put up her hand and said, "Me: I remember me." What a beautiful answer, but it enabled the Bishop to explain tactfully that growing up means getting away from the "me" and becoming concerned with others.

* * *

One way of building up community, is to have "house groups" in a parish. In the late 1960s I instigated this amongst the RAF families in Cyprus, centring them in the celebration of the Mass – until I was told to stop by the Bishop to the Forces.

However, back in civilian life, I found our diocesan bishop quite in favour and a thriving parish community was created mainly through small groups of people in the different neighbourhoods and villages coming together each month for the Eucharist, a study topic and some light refreshment.

* * *

In the RA Expeditions, Thor Heyerdahl recounts how, for two months, seven men lived together peacefully on a small papyrus boat: seven men from seven nations – Thor Heyerdahl from Norway; Carlo Mauri from Italy – film photographer; Santiago Genoves from Mexico, quartermaster; Norman Baker from USA, navigator; Georges Gourial from Egypt, underwater expert; Yugi Senkevich from Russia, ship's doctor; Abdullah Djibrine from Chad, papyrus expert. Muslim, Jewish and Christian, Capitalist and Communist.

★ ★ ★

Sometimes in a group or community it is necessary to stop and review four areas: strengths, weaknesses, opportunities and threats: SWOT's.

★ ★ ★

An eminent psychologist once said that men's greatest problem was dissociation. When Hull was a University College in the 1950s, Principal Nicholson would frequently address the 800 odd students who were there at the time, invariably including in his remarks the phrase, "We are a community," and the tone of his voice would ascend on the first four syllables and descend suddenly to a bass tone on the second syllable of "community". My subsequent life has been haunted by that phrase.

★ ★ ★

As I mentioned before, it has been said that loneliness is the greatest suffering in our western society. However, it is something we have brought on ourselves. Some people do not wish to share with others, and it is true that we all need space and time to be still and quiet. Some who live alone, including today the large majority of clergy, claim that they like it that way and are not lonely and, as a result, do not become selfish.......but I wonder............

However, opening our homes to others, especially if we live alone and have more than one spare bedroom, can be an enriching experience and could also help to alleviate the housing shortage.

* * *

A hug
Feels good
Dispels loneliness
Overcomes fears
Builds self-esteem (Wow! They actually want to hug me!)
Slows down aging, huggers stay younger longer
Eases tension
Fights insomnia
Keeps arms and shoulder muscles in condition
Is ecologically sound, does not upset the environment
Is democratic, anyone is eligible for a hug
Is portable
Affirms physical being
Is energy efficient, saves heat
Makes impossible days possible
Makes happier days happier
A hug makes you feel good all day

* * *

Weddings can be very different. Once I had a couple who were travelling people. I had learned to be prepared for anything, recalling a baptism of several years previously, when the children present all hung around the font with their hands dipped in the water and both adults and children charismatically replying to every phrase I uttered.

In the case of the wedding I had impressed on the bride and bridegroom the importance of arriving on time at 11.30 a.m. as I had to attend a meeting in the next town at 1 o'clock. However, travelling folk have little idea of time and it was 12.20 p.m. before all were present and ready, with their glittering bangles and rings and cheap but smart dresses smelling of body odour and the breaths of many of the men smelling of drink. Innumerable children between the ages of 3 and 10 provided a continuous background of noise as they ran around the altar, slid on the benches and scattered confetti everywhere. Nothing I said to try to stop them made any impression and at times their voices gained ascendancy over my own.

The organist afterwards said he felt very sorry for me. I felt sorry for myself, too, and rather depressed, wondering whether I should have continued in view of the state of some who came up for Holy Communion.

Two days later I read in the local paper: "Following a Roman Catholic wedding in the Cathedral tiny tearaways at a gypsy wedding reception created havoc at a Northampton pub. Police were called in after about 70 children set off fire extinguishers, ripped lavatory fittings from the walls and got into the cellar and removed the bungs from the beer barrels!"

* * *

By contrast to this, was one of the happiest weddings at which I ever officiated. The young couple were both going to do voluntary service overseas and they had decided, against their parents wishes, to have a very simple celebration. Ten people were present, including parents and a few very close relatives. There were no extra flowers in the side chapel of the Cathedral where I celebrated the nuptial Mass; no music and they were dressed in t-shirts and jeans.

At first I thought it would be difficult to make a really joyful celebration, but I was mistaken. Their love and joy just shone out from them and it was infectious. They then followed the church service with a simple meal in a nearby pub.

This does not mean to imply that it has to be simple in order to be joyful. Evidence of this was Katie and Henrik's wedding in Sweden at which we were all dressed up and experienced lots of extras, but, again, the love of the couple radiated out from them and was in no way swamped by the accessories. These, in fact, became an amusing distraction to holiday-makers on the island of Marstrand where the Reception took place. Many of the male guests were in morning dress (I was in a black suit and Roman collar) and during the ten-minute walk along the harbour front to the Sodra Strandverkat for the reception we wove our way through gazing crowds of lightly and sometimes scantily-dressed holiday makers.

⋆ ⋆ ⋆

A small girl was once taken to her first wedding ceremony and afterwards she turned to her mother and said, "I think that lady changed her mind: she went up the aisle with one man, and came down with another."

⋆ ⋆ ⋆

Teams of Our Lady, somewhat a misnomer as it sounds better in the original French "Equipes de Notre Dame," is a worldwide movement which seeks to help married couples develop their spirituality – their relationship with God, personally, and as a couple with their community. A team usually comprises four to six couples with, if possible, a priest, or nun. They meet monthly, sharing a meal and their news – the highs, the lows, the delights and stresses. They have a time of prayer together, discuss a study topic and review their lives from a spiritual angle – daily prayer, Bible reading, time together each month as a couple when they can open up to each other, - this is known as "the sit down".

In November 1992 before ever being linked with a specific team, I was invited to Badby, near Daventry, for a national gathering of representatives of teams drawn from around the country. I was asked to be a Sector Chaplain. It was from this that we soon generated a number of teams in the Northampton area. The commitment and the structure of the monthly meetings appealed to me. Little did I think then, that fifteen years later I would be the Super-Regional Chaplain, covering various countries of the Transatlantic Super Region: South Africa, Trindad, Malawi, Ireland, Scotland and Austria!

★ ★ ★

I have been Team's chaplain of a local team, either in Northampton or Little Chalfont for many years now, and, for a short time I took part in several French Team meetings in Ealing. At one of these the discussion was led by a young French wife who, whilst declaiming on some quite complex subject, stood up, picked up her baby who was on a cushion on the floor in the corner of the room, and started walking to and fro with the baby sucking at her breast. I was so intrigued by all this that I have completely forgotten on what profound theological topic she was continuing to expound!

* * *

Marriages can sometimes be put to the test. There was the case of the man who one day arrived at work looking gloomy, depressed and irritable.

"What's up?" his colleague asked him.

"My wife," he replied, "reversed the car out of the garage this morning."

"Well, what's unusual about that?"

"Well, you see, I reversed it in last night."

* * *

At a Teams of Our Lady international gathering at Santiago de Campostello in September 2000, one of the greatest highlights, as far as the conference was concerned was the talk by Dr Jack Dominian. He and his wife Edith had come over on the Monday and stayed until the Thursday. I got to know them quite well during this time.

At the conference on the Wednesday Jack had a standing ovation which went on for several minutes. I said to him that evening "Have you ever had such a big audience so appreciative before?" because there were over eight thousand of us, and his talk was met with such tremendous enthusiasm. Compared with the French presentations it was more pragmatic and on the wavelength of everybody there. There would certainly be some French theorists who would have not thought it so good, but the vast majority were talking about it for the rest of the week. We English bathed in reflected glory.

I remarked to Jack's wife, Edith, that she should have added perhaps a few words as well. "Oh" she replied "I did in fact write a few paragraphs. I had my say." They were a wonderful couple, in their mid seventies.

⋆ ⋆ ⋆

One of the couples in our Little Chalfont Team of Our Lady, Jon and Roseann Rogers, mentioned in the course of our monthly meeting, that they had found a certain book by an American Gary Chapman both interesting and useful on the subject of marriage. The title – "The Five Love Languages."

It turned out to be easy reading and explained the five ways in which love can be expressed. I lent it recently to Dr Jack Dominian, who thought it so good that he felt that it should be published here in the UK. So, in what way might it be helpful to us?

There are, writes Gary Chapman, five principal ways in which we show our love to others – and he has written other books applying this to single people, children, teenagers and our relationship to God.

The first language of love is that of words of affirmation. "The tongue has the power of life and death." Words of encouragement, kind words, words of forgiveness and reconciliation are all important in our loving relationships. Then there is the quality time given to one's partner, and without actually using Teams's terminology, he writes of the significance of the "sit-down". Receiving gifts is a third way, and if this is your spouse's primary love language, you can become a proficient gift giver and this is one of the easiest love languages to learn. Acts of service to one another, and finally, physical touch complete the picture. The latter includes holding hands, hugging, kissing, intercourse, although the last is only one dialect in the love language of touch.

It is important to know what one's primary love language is, and, usually husband and wife will differ in this. It is even more important to know what one's partner's primary love language is and then be able to make an effort to fulfil it.

The book is full of examples from Gary Chapman's experience of counselling married couples. He cites, for example, the case of the husband who spends most of his spare time playing football, when his wife's primary language is "quality time", time she wants to just be with her husband. He needs to realise this and she, in her turn, perhaps needs to know that her husband needs, most of all, encouragement and affirmation.

The book concludes with a questionnaire for both husbands and wives to help them determine what their primary love language is. In short, then, I wholeheartedly recommend this series of books to everyone.

★ ★ ★

Charles and Irene Bazeley celebrated their Diamond wedding anniversary with a Mass at which they renewed their wedding vows and invited me to join them for a celebration in a nearby hotel-restaurant. Towards the end of the meal Alan, their son, rose to his feet to express his appreciation of his parents. Charles, who was, even at the age of eighty, a good six-footer, and was clearly very moved by the whole occasion, stood up, and almost choking with emotion, replied to his son's kind words, in the course of which he said, looking down on Irene seated at his side, "Well, do you know, I think I can honestly say we've never in all that time had a quarrel – have we, Irene?" She looked up at him, gave a little smile, and added, "Well no, just a few differences of opinion!"

* * *

Queen Marie-Therese in Austria had sixteen children and wanted to marry them all off to royal families in different countries in Europe. Marie-Antoinette, who was beheaded during the French Revolution, was one of them. Maybe this expressed a desire for European Union!

* * *

Television and computers do not always make the best contribution to family life. They can become "electronic baby-sitters" for many children who miss out on family life. They are "screen kids", and many watch TV during the evening meal. They also, in showing families at odds with one another; fighting, shouting, swearing – good drama – but this gives an impression that this is the norm.

* * *

The following was one of several early morning radio talks, "Lift up Your Hearts", which I was asked to give, and I include it because it illustrates the need of family guidance

Good Morning! Have you ever been offered chewing-gum for breakfast? – I have! Some years ago when I was chaplain in the RAF and worked quite a lot with young families, a young lad of 9 came to my office carrying an enormous paper bag which turned out to be full of packets of chewing gum.

"Have one, Father" he said.

I asked him where he'd got it all from.

"From the NAAFI shop," he said.

I found out later that he'd pinched the lot!

So, after talking to him, I went to see his parents, and found that this was just one of the many bad habits he'd got into in order to attract attention to himself.

Fortunately for him and everyone concerned, the NAAFI manager agreed to take no action in the matter.

Later we managed to get the youngster involved in the cubs and various other activities, the parents co-operated, and soon he began to grow out of his dishonest habits.

This isn't an uncommon situation, is it?

There are all sorts of reasons why a child will steal chewing-gum, or money, or anything else.....it's not always to attract attention! It may be because he is very young, and doesn't distinguish very well between what is his and what belongs to someone else. Perhaps he isn't given pocket money, while his pals have plenty. Or perhaps he's deprived of affection (or, at least, thinks he is) and so he steals by way of compensation. He's punished, and then he thinks that he's rejected even more, and so he goes stealing again (ie steals all the more) to console himself.

Or, again, he may want very badly a particular toy, and he feels sure that his parents will refuse to buy it for him, so he takes money from his father's wallet to pay for it. An older lad may, of course, be going through a period of revolt and rebellion against his parents, and so he steals out of revenge.

These may be some of the reasons why a child is dishonest. If you are a parent, what should you do about it?

Or, what can I, as a priest, do about it?

Most important of all, we should never treat children as thieves and humiliate them in public. The training begins, doesn't it, in the very earliest years when the child learns that some things are his, and some are not; and that there's a very close connection between money and work. And from about the age of 7, it's probably good that a child has at least a little pocket money of his own.

If it's a question of punishing a child after stealing, then we must always be constructive about it. The answer may be to reduce the pocket-money for a while, or the ration of sweets, but after that, to treat the child as if nothing had happened. To start locking up everything is hardly ever the answer.

Most important of all, we ourselves must be absolutely honest, if we are to expect and help others to be. So much depends on the good example of us all, but especially you, who are parents, in this all-important task of guiding, and helping, and leading a child to have the right attitudes, and to grow up, as my chewing-gum friend did, into an open and honest individual.

May God bless us all, and help us in this task.

* * *

Community in the family can be greatly helped through prayer and religious education guided and led by parents. This in part inspired me to instigate a system of family catechetics whilst I was at Bedford. The following is an account of this as it appeared in an article I wrote for The Clergy Review in 1973.

In July 1970 several happenings conspired together to generate a scheme of catechetics designed to help children attending non-Catholic schools, and at the same time providing an opportunity of further education for adults.

Some months previously I had been posted to a fairly mixed "wedge" parish in Bedford. Most of the Catholic population came from a new housing estate area in the town, but in addition to this there were nine villages, one of which was large enough to have 80 Catholic families. In spite of very good Catholic schools in the town, many children, through lack of school space, attended local non-Catholic schools, and this was, in any case of course, the only answer in the country areas. The local parish church was newly built on the housing estate, and because of the considerable debt on it, no parish hall or presbytery existed. This meant that for nearly an hour every Saturday morning, approximately seventy children aged 4½ to 11 years huddled into groups around the church, in the gallery, the sacristy and any other odd corners to be found, for their catechism class. The result of this, in spite of the heroic efforts of the group of catechists and teachers who took the groups, was pretty chaotic. Only two children came in from the country each week and the rest were attending non-Catholic schools in the town area.

My dissatisfaction with this state of affairs was shared by our catechists, who were mostly teachers at the Catholic school, together with one of the sisters from the nearby convent. And then two articles in The Clergy Review (July 1970) stirred up thoughts about the importance of educating parents so that they could educate their own children. This seemed to be the logical answer. I discussed it with the catechists and with the sisters at the convent. I discussed it with a sprinkling of the parents concerned. With some hesitations, they all thought it was a good idea, at least worth trying, and anyway, anything would surely be better than the present set-up!

It then occurred to me that we, priest, sisters and teachers, were quite suddenly going to have virtually no contact at all with the children, and this, while not being disastrous, would certainly be a pity. We were going from one extreme to another, from dealing uniquely with the children, we were now proposing to deal only with the parents. Surely this could not be a good thing. From this conviction there grew the idea of combining the two systems, and it was, I think, in this respect that our scheme was unique. (Cambridge since adopted a similar scheme.) We decided to involve both parents and children (5 to 11-year-olds) in one fell swoop: to instruct and help the parents, and at the same time see and help the children.

Our small group of three sisters, four lay teachers, two of whom had families of their own, met for a whole day, and we, with tears, sweat and heart-searchings, hammered out in detail the scheme that follows.

We decided that our basic aim was to help parents instruct their own children in the knowledge and love of Christ, the elements of the faith, and how to prepare the children for the sacraments. In this way they would be fulfilling effectively the promises contained in the Baptismal rite; they would become closer to their children in the very things that are essential to a happy and fulfilled Christian life; and finally, they would themselves be better informed on questions connected with their faith – particularly important in these days of constant and rapid growth and change.

The scheme was to be primarily for those with children aged 5 to 11 years attending non-Catholic schools, but it was emphasised that it would also be most useful for any others who wished to attend, and in fact we have found that there are always a few parents, with offspring at Catholic schools, who come as well. In future we hope to make it clear that the adult sessions would be useful and helpful for anyone.

In practice, it means that ideally the whole family come for 1¼ hours on a Saturday afternoon once a month – it actually works out at about ten sessions in the year, allowing for the holidays. The meetings are held in various rooms and halls in the nearby convent, which is in fact the Provincial House of the Daughters of the Holy Ghost, and fairly conveniently situation in relation to both town and villages.

A topic is chosen for each month, which parents and children, the latter divided into age groups, consider separately. The parents deal with the topic for the ensuing month, while the children have a project on the topic for the preceding month.

The Parents: the session for the parents, who are free from the worry of their children, begins with a general background talk on the topic for the month ahead, usually given by myself. This is then followed by a second talk by one of the catechists on how best to apply all this to the practical level of the children of different ages. The parents then sometimes have a general question/discussion period, or break up into smaller groups for discussion and then feed-back.

The Children: 0-4½ years: looked after separately by some teenage girls; 4½ to 11 years: divided into groups according to age, with a teacher who reviews with them what they have done in the preceding month, and develops a project on the subject. Separate children's groups are, of course, formed prior to the reception of the sacraments, and half-day retreats also augment the help given by the parents.

The children join their parents for the last five minutes and lead a short and simple service.

To support the scheme, we have prepared leaflets which are available each month. These comprise a general summary of the given topic for the parents, together with more practical leaflets on how to apply this for the children in the different age groups. A two-year syllabus is being followed, and the monthly topics are naturally as closely linked as possible with the liturgical year. Families unable to come to the monthly sessions may collect the leaflets after Mass on Sunday, and we are, in this third year of the scheme, beginning a system of visiting of the parents by the catechists, particularly with a view to helping and encouraging a minority who, for various reasons, have not been attending.

The emphasis throughout, is not to transfer the catechism class from church to home, but rather, to permeate the whole atmosphere of the home with the spirit of Christ, and help parents to find informal "hooks", as it were, on which to hang the topic for the month. The arrangement of house groups and Masses throughout the parish also helps considerably in all this. Furthermore, recently, we have started another scheme, necessarily of a different nature, for the 11 to 18 year-olds, but this is still in its early experimental stages.

It would be impossible to sum up, after only two years, the results of the scheme. All one can say at this stage is that while a few have dropped by the wayside, finding it too much for them to cope with, the majority of parents have begun to discover, through both learning themselves and teaching their children, that the love of God and their neighbour is not a departmentalized thing in their lives, but is something that should impregnate the whole of it, and be continually in a state of growth and development. It is something that affects the whole atmosphere of the family, and this is why the family and the relationships of love within it, provide the ideal setting for introducing a child to the Truth that is Christ, and all that following him implies.

Non-Catholic husbands have, as a result of the scheme, been found to open the Bible and help their child find various passages about Our Lord, and even come to Mass with them. In many families it has been a means of breaking down barriers. "Something is happening in our family because of this," said one parent. A Catholic father whose only point of contact with his 10-year-old son had been football, suddenly found that he could converse with him on a wide range of other subjects, too.

Furthermore, children seem to have been very well prepared for the sacraments of Penance and Communion, the latter which they receive with the rest of their family, each family approaching the altar separately. And as far as the adult education is concerned, many admit that they wouldn't attend if they didn't have to for the sake of their children.

So then, we have seen over these two years, that while there are disadvantages to the scheme, for nothing is perfect, these are nevertheless far outweighed by the advantages. The parents here fell in with the scheme remarkably quickly and well. It could be more difficult in other areas. In Cambridge, where it is organised on a town basis, a general meeting of all parents concerned about the problem was held, and the proposed scheme explained to them before it was actually launched. This is certainly preferable to the more autocratic launching that it had in this parish!

FAMILY CATECHETICS: A PARENT'S EXPERIENCE

My family and I Iive in a village near Bedford and my daughter attends the local non-Catholic school. In 1970, when she was seven, I became increasingly concerned that she should be prepared for her first Holy Communion. I made enquiries and heard that a new scheme was to begin shortly at the nearby convent, which would assist parents in the religious instruction of their children, and would also take account of children who were preparing for the sacraments. It was in this way that I became involved in the scheme.

The implication that my wife and I should be totally responsible for my daughter's religious instruction was a little daunting, but nevertheless we thought that the scheme was worth a try. We had both received the conventional Catholic school education, and although we considered ourselves a bit rusty in this sphere, we imagined that a refresher course in the catechism combined with guidance in instruction technique would suffice for our needs. From the first meeting, however, we learned that there was a new approach to catechetics which involved more than a speedy refresher course on the catechism, and soon realised that this scheme was a comprehensive means of meeting our parental responsibilities in a practical way, guided by Fr. Payne, the sisters, and the lay catechists.

The sequence of events at the meetings was described in the previous article – the instruction session for the parents, followed by the catechist's guidance on the future month's work, and finally the parents' discussion groups. He also described how the children were simultaneously receiving instruction and talking to the sisters about their previous month's efforts. It must be understood, however, that these meetings are not an end in themselves, but are the preparation for the day-by-day involvement of parents and children in the scheme. I would like to give an account of the meetings from the parents' point of view.

Fr Payne's instruction session on the month's topic, usually related to the events of the liturgical year, is intended to inform the parents, and to provide sufficient background information to enable them to answer their children's queries. The talk is at an adult level and has the effect of making one think again about the truths of our religion. On occasion some of his remarks tend to startle the listener, who has felt so secure in the convictions acquired during childhood. This may be expected when it is considered that the talks are bridging the gap for people like myself between childhood education and the post Vatican II approach to catechetics. The net result is to stimulate the parents into discussion of their own views and differences in the later discussion session. I may also add that it has made us aware of the gaps in our religious knowledge.

The second stage in which the catechist explains the parents' guidelines and children's leaflets is very helpful. The catechists are parents and one cannot fail to realise that their explanation of the suggested approach to the month's work is influenced by their own experience as parents. The emphasis in this part is that the material in the guidelines' leaflet is the suggested approach and it is fully understood that parents are free to adopt this approach or not, according to their experience of their children's ability to absorb the information. In practice each parent adapts the guidance on the leaflets to the needs of their own children.

In the discussion stage the parents have the opportunity to state their own views, seek additional information, and express any doubts they may have on anything that has been said in the instruction talk. In short, this is the time when parents have their say. The most valuable part of this interchange of views is that we learn from each other. It is reassuring to know that other people have the same problems as oneself and to discover how they cope with them. My only misgiving on this part of the meeting is the lack of time; a common feature of most discussions.

My daughter seems to be very happy with her activities during the meeting and developed an affection for the sisters who take these sessions. It is worth noting that she would probably have never made this contact with the nuns had we not become involved with the scheme.

In the ensuing month my wife and I put what we have learned into practice by attempting to make the instruction as enjoyable as possible and avoiding formality. The instruction can take the form of reading the recommended passages of scripture together, or practical work such as colouring maps of the Holy Land, or perhaps my daughter composing her own prayers. Often our sessions are simply conversations when out walking, or even no more than one answer to one question. The month's work on the leaflets is not always completed in time for the next meeting, because I find it better to establish our own pace rather than to finish the leaflet for its own sake. This results in a natural attitude to the subject and makes it easy on parent as well as child.

In conclusion I feel that the scheme is a good one for parents in our circumstances and I look forward to the extension of the scheme which will include the needs of my teenage sons.

Reg Baxter
84 Neville Crescent
Bromham, Beds

* * *

Finally, under the heading of "Community", our response to God's love must include the place of the priest in the community of the parish. I quote from Pastor Ignotus in the Tablet in 2001.

Yet another parish is to be left priestless. This has been coming for some time. Since 1989 it has been evident that about a third of parishes in this country would be priestless by 2005.

Having spent nearly two thirds of my life working all hours, visiting the sick, rushing to bedsides, hearing confessions, celebrating Masses and preparing homilies, I find it undermining that the system appears not to be bothered to replace me. It's demoralising to have to tell people, who have been daily Mass-goers for decades, that Masses are being cut – but not to fuss about it because millions of Catholics get only a couple of Masses a year.

We've spent generations preaching "It's the Mass that matters" and inculcating frequent communion, the need for confession and the risks of dying without the sacrament, only to have the Church itself call the importance of all this into question. One morning, years ago, I was in the bath when the doorbell rang. I came down to find that whoever had rung the bell had gone. I discovered it had been a man searching for a priest for his dying father. The distress haunts me still. Yet dying without the sacraments will become the norm.

No wonder lay people spit disdain when we priests tell them that the crisis in vocations is their fault, because their children should have become priests or nuns. They know good priests who have left the ministry and have to sit in the congregation while other priests are rushing from pillar to post. They see bishops hampered in developing a missionary Church and overwhelmed by priests problems.

Lay people have seen their lives and their work transformed in the past 50 years; they have seen their children grow up in a different world. They cannot understand why the Church should maintain its old model of priesthood – a model so evidently in a state of collapse.

Lay people know that celibacy itself does not cause paedophilia or any other deviancy. But they are concerned that celibacy skews recruitment. They know many mature family men (some already ordained) who would make brilliant priests. They can see why the younger generation is not tempted to join "a declining and ageing profession."

From the election of Stephen in Acts, to the choosing of well-rounded, mature and experienced family men in the Pastoral Epistles: from the decision to give elders the role of presiding in remote areas in place of bishops at the Eucharist; to the selection by the people of priests from among the mature married men of the parish; from the early medieval introduction of a monastic model of celibate priest, the development of religious priests whose only authority was in the confessional: from the model of autocratic clergyman in the baroque alliance of throne and altar, to the nineteenth-century model of priest as a sacred person set apart from the world for sacred work – the Church has over the years readily adapted priestly ministry to the changing pastoral needs of the faithful.

Over the past 50 years, however, the Church has brought about an unprecedented theological shift: it has placed the priority of the pastoral needs of the people and the Eucharistic identity of the Church below a particular historically conditioned model of ordained ministry.

The results are disastrous. Well over 50 per cent of parishes, or quasi-parishes, worldwide are now priestless. Even where vocations are increasing, they cannot keep pace with the growing numbers of Catholics – and even the urbanisation is leading to a collapse in both priestly ministry and faith. Granted, the Church has attempted to alleviate the problem with lay ministries; but ironically lay ministry flourishes where there are no priests and wilts under priestly authority. Plainly our model of priest is not only dying: it is dysfunctional.

Lay participation in the Church's mission is not about more lay people and fewer priests, but rather about authentic Eucharistic and evangelising communities needing more of both.

Perpetuating the old model of priesthood means we are becoming a non-eucharistic, de-sacramentalised Church, bereft of authorised preaching. But the authorities will still not permit an open and honest discussion.

I have a recurrent nightmare; at the fifty-ninth minute of the eleventh hour, I am running down a terraced street – every house a heavenly mansion. I am trying to open each door in turn, but someone shuts it in my face: "You can't come in; I was hungry and you told me there was no Mass till next year," "I was sick and my urgent message got lost in an endless loop of answering machines," "I was naked and raw with grief and you did not have time", I was dying but I could only cry out 'My God, my God why have you forsaken me'".

Eventually, in despair, I fall through a door at the feet of a young lone mother who has struggled to offer some life and dignity to her children. She lets me in, saying: "You too are a victim – of institutions blind to the wrong they've caused. Come! Enter the peace of the Lord."

As a conclusion to this chapter on community one should mention the importance for all of us, and especially Christians, of coming together to lead the way in combating global warming through the reduction of carbon emissions, the planting of trees, making use of wind power, installing water-efficient toilets and, in particular, ground-source heating in churches, halls and groups of houses. Furthermore, urged by the world economic crisis, if nothing else, we must learn to live more simply so that others may simply live.

* * *

The final step of Love and Rebirth

The one great certainty in our lives is that of our death, although the circumstances surrounding it are unknown to us, and we may be quite fearful at the thought of it. However, everyday of our lives, indeed every moment is a death-moment: death to the past and rebirth to the future.

This makes the present moment the most important for us. This ongoing present moment is where we strike eternity, which is not 'another place' or 'forever and ever' or time stretching on and on. It is a spring. Henri Boulad in his fantastic book "All is Grace: man and the mystery of time" writes of the interchange within the Trinity which makes God an ever-flowing spring in the infinite wonder of self-giving.

That's quite profound but, again, it underlines the fact that the only thing that really matters is our intense experience of the present. Death and rebirth then become one.

⋆ ⋆ ⋆

My father, who lived to be 99 years old, suffered a shrapnel wound in his right arm during the First World War. As a result of this he could no longer play the piano, except with one hand, and had to learn to write with his left hand. In middle age he became quite deaf and then in his early seventies partially sighted which prevented him from reading.

However, in spite of these disabilities, about which I never once heard him complain, he, in his nineties, had his memoirs published, "The Chronicle of a Century", and I recall one evening at supper someone asked him if there had been anything special on the news. My father immediately listed five news headlines and then threw the weather forecast in to make weight!

When asked for the secret of being so fit in old age, he would invariably reply: "Punctuality, regularity, and moderation in all things," and he certainly put this into practice.

⋆ ⋆ ⋆

A little girl was once asked how old she was and she replied, "I'm not old at all, I'm nearly new!"

⋆ ⋆ ⋆

Two boys were playing noisily in their grandmother's room when they suddenly noticed that she was reading her bible.

"We'd better by quiet," remarked the older one, "Grandma's swotting for her finals."

* * *

"When I was young, I knew what was wrong with the world; in middle age, I knew what was wrong with those around me; and now that I am old, I can see what is wrong with me" (Source unknown)

* * *

Les Ladbrooke once spotted an old acquaintance in a railway station. "My dear Landerson!" he cried. "How you've changed! You look younger – your face is round, you've got good colour, you've shaved off your moustache – my, how you've changed." The bewildered man stared at Ladbrooke. But my name isn't Landerson," he remarked. "What?" Ladbrooke replied, "Changed your name, too?"

* * *

Once upon a time a little boy lived with his parents, poor peasants, in a simple hut in the woods. The parents loved their child, and he returned their love and was a good son to them. Also living with this family was the grandfather of the little boy. He was old and frail and no longer able to work. He sat all day in his chair, and when he came to table he was so shaky that he could hardly eat, and made a great deal of mess around his place. One day his trembling hand caused him to drop and break his platter and spill all the food on the ground.

The boy's mother was furious. She shouted at the poor old man, shook him and said that henceforth he would eat all his meals from a wooden bowl as he was not fit to eat from a plate like normal people.

Ashamed and humiliated, the old man withdrew from the table to the corner, where, isolated and lonely, he ate only from a wooden bowl like a baby.

One day his parents noticed the little boy busy with a knife and a block of wood. "What are you doing? What are you making?" they asked.

"I'm making bowls for you both to eat out of, when you are old", he answered in his simplicity.

(Origin unknown)

* * *

As one heads towards death and rebirth it is good to reflect on one's life, and what follows is a brief personal account of my life as a priest.

For the first five years after ordination I was curate in a parish where the resident housekeeper boasted that she was really almost the curate and could do most things except say Mass and give Absolution! Every Monday the whole morning was taken up helping the parish priest count the money; homes were systematically visited; ecumenism consisted of a cup of tea and cake together annually with clergy of other denominations, in the week of prayer for Christian unity; classes were taken in the Catholic school, with extra classes for those attending the non-Catholic grammar school; hospital and sick visiting fell entirely to the priest; and apart from the Legion of Mary and the SVP, meetings of any sort were rare.

The effects of Vatican II began to be felt by 1966 and by then I was a chaplain in the RAF, spending nearly three years in Cyprus. The renewed emphasis on the importance of Scripture and the Liturgy of the Word coincided with regularly leading pilgrimages to the Holy Land. This was a major step forward in appreciating much more the life of the Lord and his teaching. Furthermore, being inserted, as it were, in the organisation of the RAF, I rapidly learnt the importance of allowing others to use their skills for the more material aspects of Church administration. This has stood me in good stead ever since.

On returning to pastoral work in the Northampton diocese, I was parish priest in a parish on the edge of Bedford which included nine villages. As mentioned previously, House Groups were started up throughout the parish and I realised the value of sharing in a small group without too much structure. Most of the groups at that time involved a monthly celebration of a "house Mass". This was continued, to a lesser degree, when I moved to Aylesbury, although there the keynote of ministry developed into the form of welcoming. The fairly large presbytery was an open house to all – the homeless, students, the sick, the foreigner; those with "a problem", as well as others who were employed in a profession. All were welcome, and for much of the time, some six to eight people were together in the house. Some stayed a week or two, others up to several years, and some became involved in the pastoral work of the town centre parish.

Then, for thirteen years I was Administrator or Dean at Northampton Cathedral. This, like most of life's experiences, had both its negative and positive aspects. The welcoming ministry had to be more restricted; the focus had to be on the deanery and the diocese as well as the parish and this I did not find easy. Although many of the administrative tasks were spread around amongst many good and willing volunteers, there was still much left for me to deal with. However, the ecumenical activities flourished, various new style groups were encouraged, such as a Bereavement Support Group, Spirituality and contemplative prayer groups, Youth 2000, and Teams of Our Lady. Throughout the Church much more importance was given to preparation for receiving the Sacraments, and, through a fortuitous series of events, I became very involved in the third world dimension in the form of supporting The Missionaries of the Poor in the various areas of their work with the homeless and the destitute in Jamaica, India and the Philippines. In all this work at the Cathedral, I was encouraged and supported by my father, who lived with me and, until he died at the healthy age of 99 years, was more like an older brother, and a magnet to many in both the parish and the diocese.

Latterly, in the much smaller parish of St Aidan's, Little Chalfont, some of the positive aspects of my ministry as a priest over the past years have been once again highlighted. These include the prime importance of welcome and hospitality in the lives of all Christians, and especially within the Catholic parish and presbytery. Cardinal Martini, at one of the Synod of Bishops in Rome said that "the parish should become a sign of communion and hope for the world, offering a credible alternative to a fragmented society and ethics." The small committed group, - base communities, Teams,etc – as part of a parish, I see as essential in helping to create this communion and hope for those around us, for unbelievers and those who have abandoned religious practice. Meanwhile, I find that I am fortunate to have inherited a parochial structure in which the general administration and the maintenance of the parish is taken care of by a number of "lay co-ordinators", each with a small team of people to help. Personally, I see the ultimate authority in these areas falling on competent and trained laity, so that the priest does not necessarily have the final say. He becomes much more, as he is in Teams, a chaplain, a minister of the Word of God "to promote, animate and preserve unity and to open up to the needs and dynamism of the Church" This has given me time in the past few years to indulge in a little writing – a further means of, I hope, spreading God's word in a situation that has changed a great deal since I was first ordained.

⋆ ⋆ ⋆

"Try to squeeze from all ugliness at least one or two drops of clear beauty. It is there if you will only look for it" (From "Learn to Laugh again" by Oliver Sandys.)

⋆ ⋆ ⋆

I walked around the Parc de Jean-Paul II. This used to be the seminary garden situated in the banlieu of Paris. I became nostalgic as I recalled so well how I used to walk around that same perimeter, often at night before going to bed, looking at the distant lights of the city and listening to the faint far-off sounds of life.

The avenue of trees was unchanged but part of the parc had been cut off from what had been the building where we seminarists had studied philosophy. It now seemed to be sold off for other more secular uses. In the centre of this building had been the small chapel, known to M. Olier and where I had celebrated my very first Mass in the presence of a small group of friends before leaving for England and the first 'proper' Mass at Sutton Park, near Guildford.

The changes made me sad.

⋆ ⋆ ⋆

We live in a world of change, and Christians throughout the centuries have experienced change within the Church. I had the good fortune to be trained as a priest by seminary professors in France who were, several years before Vatican II, teaching and putting into effect much of what that Council later propagated.

Thus it was that when I returned to England it felt as if I had taken a few steps backwards, and I recall that one day a few weeks after my ordination, at lunch in Cathedral House, where I was temporarily stationed, the question came up of life after death and limbo, a place of natural happiness for unbaptised babies. Quoting what I had learned in the seminary, I joined in the conversation by stating that limbo was only a theological opinion and had never been the dogmatic teaching of the Church. There was a deadly silence and I could feel the elderly and very traditional Canon Malone, seated at the head of the table, draw in his breath before exploding in a kind of apoplectic fit against the heretical teaching of the seminary.

After lunch one of the curates advised me to keep quiet in future about limbo and anything else I had learned that might be contentious!

⋆ ⋆ ⋆

A great religious leader once said that there are only three fundamental questions in which everyone is interested:

- Where have I come from?
- Where am I going?
- How am I to get there?

* * *

A man found an eagle's egg and put it in the nest of a backyard hen. The eaglet hatched with the brood of chicks and grew up with them.

All his life the eagle did what the backyard chickens did, thinking he was a backyard chicken. He scratched the earth for worms and insects. He clucked and cackled. And he would thrash his wings and fly a few feet into the air like the chickens. After all, that is how a chicken is supposed to fly, isn't it?

Years passed and the eagle grew very old. One day he saw a magnificent bird far above him in the cloudless sky. It floated in graceful majesty among thc powerful wind currents, with scarcely a beat of the strong golden wings.

The old eagle looked up in awe. "Who's that?" he said to his neighbour.

"That's the eagle, the king of the birds," said his neighbour. "But don't give it another thought. You and I are different from him.

So the eagle never gave it another thought. He died thinking he was a backyard chicken.

* * *

What does man love more than life?
Fears more than death or mortal strife?
The rich man needs; the poor man has
The miser gives, the spendthrift saves
And all men carry to their graves?
["Nothing"]

* * *

An Englishman, Scotsman and Irishman were discussing what was the greatest invention in the world.

The Englishman claimed it was the heart transplant: "Otherwise," he said "it would be curtains for me."

The Scotsman disagreed: "Ooch, no it'd be a liver transplant – otherwise curtains for me."

To this the Irishman responded: "The greatest invention in the world would be Venetian blinds – otherwise curtains for everyone!"

* * *

In "Lady Windermere's Fan" by Oscar Wilde, Lady Windermere speaks of the materialism of Victorian England and goes on to say that the ideal of life is love and its purification is through sacrifice.

* * *

The consultant surgeon told Basil that an operation could prolong his life by possibly a couple of months, but that was all. This information was pronounced coldly and abruptly and concluded with the question, "Well, do you want me to operate?" to which Basil opened his eyes and replied, "I wouldn't let you cut my toe nails!"

Basil died soon after this conversation and when I was visiting him for the last time, I found myself quoting the words of Peter Pan that dying is a very great adventure. However, as I said this I wondered if it was perhaps inappropriate at that moment. I need not have worried, for Basil looked at me with a brightness in his eyes and a half smile on his face and said with great conviction and faith, "Yes, it is."

* * *

Teilhard de Chardin once wrote: "When the signs of age begin to mark my body (and still more, when they touch my mind); when the ill that is to diminish me or carry me off strikes from without or is born within me; when the painful moment comes in which I suddenly awaken to the fact that I am ill or growing old; and above all, at that last moment when I feel I am losing hold of myself and am absolutely passive within the hands of the greatest unknown forces that have formed me; in all those dark moments, O God, grant that I may understand that it is You (provided my faith is strong enough) who are painfully parting the fibres of my being, in order to penetrate to the very marrow of my substance and bear me away within Yourself........"

* * *

I was on holiday on a Greek island on the sixth September 1997. Greek television and radio were silent for 3 hours and the only broadcast was that of Princess Diana's funeral from Westminster Abbey. Several of us sat and watched it on television in one of the cafes by the sea-front at Spetses, the island she had visited just 3 weeks previously. The commentary was in Greek but we got some idea of it through the visuals and a few words here and there came through. It seemed to me that the two most moving moments were Earl Spencer's speech and Elton John's song modified especially for the occasion. Joanna, who was the English wife of a Greek who between them run the cafe where we were, put a box of kitchen tissues on the table for us all.

It was indeed very moving. Princess Diana was such a vibrant and wonderful personality. Yes, she certainly had her faults but I'm sure the good that she did far overrode them.

* * *

Cardinal Hume in a letter announcing his illness wrote "I have received two wonderful graces. First I have been given time to prepare for a new future. Secondly I find myself –uncharacteristically – calm and at peace. I intend to carry on working as much and as long as I can. I have no intention of being an invalid until I have to submit to the illness. But nevertheless I shall be a bit limited in what I can do. Above all I want no fuss. The future is in God's hands." (source unknown) I think Roger Edmunds, a good priest friend suffering from cancer, had a similar attitude of wanting to carry on as long as he could. I hope I may have that attitude when the time comes.

* * *

I was called to the hospital and found that it was for an Italian who ran a fish and chip shop locally, and who'd invited me a year or so ago to bless his house and his business, which I had duly done. He'd had a massive stroke, having been in the car, and probably feeling a little faint or sick had driven off the road, but had not been found until 2 hours later.

This was earlier in the day and by the time I arrived at the hospital, he was clearly very seriously ill indeed and his breathing was becoming more difficult. His wife was there, and his daughter and her boy-friend and another friend. I anointed him and within seconds of my giving him the Last Blessing, he rattled in his throat and breathed his last. It was dramatic and very sad for his family.

⋆ ⋆ ⋆

Lord Rosebery was very rich. He had everything. He became ill and was dying. His valet, George, asked him if he wanted the vicar. "Good God, George, no!" He then roused himself and asked for the Eton Boat song to be played on an ancient gramophone. He died to that accompaniment.

⋆ ⋆ ⋆

Walking through the streets of Pompeii, some covered in volcanic dust, I wondered if Paris and London and Rome would one day be the sign of death and destruction with future generations trying to reconstruct our present way of life: a plastic life, a throw-away life.

⋆ ⋆ ⋆

Subsequent to a severe heart attach, Don Lack remarked to me: "If the Lord wants me more up there than down here, then I'm ready to go."

⋆ ⋆ ⋆

The very nature of love involves suffering and the cross.

* * *

Joe Pilendiram, who spent a year with the Missionaries of the Poor in Kingston, recounted an experience he had on his third day of helping the Brothers:

Brother Charles came to me and asked, 'Joe, would you mind taking some clothes to Madams?' I didn't have my hearing aid at that time so I heard it as Mad Ones, so I asked him to repeat it again. He said they were the undertakers, called Madams. I thought this would be an easy job. They brought a bundle of clothes and gave them to me and I said 'I'll go and take the car'. The undertakers were behind the Public Health hospital so I went and was taken into reception. A lady received me very well – and I thought I'd just hand over the clothes and come back – until she said 'No, No, You have to identify this person who has died.' I nearly froze in my shoes because I'd taken him only once to the hospital and so I had to remember the face. The receptionist then pointed out a gentleman who was absolutely stone drunk, walking like a dog, and he led me into what I thought would be the mortuary, but as soon as I entered I saw a huge hall full of naked bodies.

I prayed to the Lord to give me strength, not for the souls who were there, but for myself. I felt like following the undertakers example and having a gin and tonic to steady myself. Anyway I prayed then for all the bodies there, and then attempted to collect my thoughts to identify this person. There was just a cloth thrown over the naked bodies. He showed me one and I said 'No' and he went on like that until I came to one whom I thought might be the one I was looking for. I came away quickly and then went to Brother Charles, 'When you sent me to deliver the clothes, you should have told me I would have to identify the body!"

⋆ ⋆ ⋆

I lead a burial service in an Anglican churchyard near Northampton. It was a pouring wet day and there had been a lot of rain overnight.

When we got to the grave, to my horror I found that it was half full of water. Apparently this was quite common in that particular village after a heavy rainfall. Fortunately the family stood fairly well back and it was possible that they did not see the water in the grave. As soon as it was appropriate I indicated that I wanted the coffin lowered so that at least it would cover up the water, but to my horror I found that the coffin seemed to be floating in it when it had been lowered. Fortunately the family were neither Irish nor Italian and so did not want to peer over and sprinkle holy water on the coffin. I for my part had suddenly realised just before the blessing of the grave that I'd left the holy water in the church, so anxious had I been to retrieve my umbrella. I decided there and then that the pouring rain would be sufficient for the blessing. However it wasn't a particularly inspiring experience seeing the coffin floating about in the water!

On another occasion in Cyprus the grave was not big enough for the coffin and I had to lead the family to the other side of the cemetery and say the rosary with them whilst the diggers got to work.

Then there was the funeral director who peered into the grave just before lowering the coffin and his spectacles fell into the hole...............

⋆ ⋆ ⋆

Dr George Hidegh-Pickler, born in Hungary, was a dentist in Aylesbury. I was the celebrant at his funeral and discovered that he had erected his own gravestone years before he died at the age of 58 through falling from a window in Stoke Mandeville hospital. Through his father he became the 26th Baron of Transylvania, and his housekeeper was quoted as saying that he was a good man to work for and that he liked everything just so, but was generous and kind – a real gentleman!

⋆ ⋆ ⋆

A good, but slightly eccentric priest of our diocese, Father David Woodard kept his coffin, already made for size, in his bedroom for many years before he died – a salutary reminder!

⋆ ⋆ ⋆

In 1993 I met up with some of the seminarians I had been with some 30 years previously. I recognised them all in spite of changes due to age; but what I noticed most were the little mannerisms, the way of smiling or laughing, of holding the head when looking at something – these had not changed at all. It was probably like this with Jesus after the Resurrection, when the disciples recognised him in the way he spoke and blessed and broke the bread.

⋆ ⋆ ⋆

The futility of ambition and climbing the ladder of success is well described in "Hope for the Flowers" by Trina Paulus where one is reminded that the most important thing in life is to be oneself and ready for that final transformation to the fullness of the afterlife. This is illustrated in the life of the caterpillar which becomes a chrysalis and eventually a butterfly. The authoress aptly describes it as "a tale – partly about life, partly about revolution, and lots about hope for adults and others (including caterpillars who can read).

It begins with the caterpillar, Stripe, emerging from an egg on a leaf, beginning to eat the leaf but soon becoming bored; "Surely there's more to life than eating?" It then noticed lots of other caterpillars making a high column reaching up to the clouds, each one struggling upwards and in doing so, stepping on others and pushing them down. No one seemed to know what was at the top. Then Stripe met Yellow and together they decided to leave the caterpillar pillar and enjoy life at the side near the bottom.

After a while, and in spite of Yellow trying to dissuade him, Stripe decided to return to the pillar. Yellow pined for him whilst he struggled upwards, being pushed down again by others, or even treading on other climbers himself.

Meanwhile, Yellow looking around her, encountered a caterpillar that was in the process of becoming a beautiful butterfly through just allowing itself seemingly to die. "Life," it explained to Yellow, "is changed, not taken away. And then," it added, "you can really love – the kind of love that makes new life."

Yellow wanted to tell Stripe all about this, but by then, she didn't know where he was, so she decided to imitate the other butterfly and spin herself with similar silky threads and change into a cocoon.

Stripe, during this time, had made progress up the caterpillar pile and he had come very near the top. There he was able to see lots of other similar pillars but above them – nothing. Then, suddenly, he saw a beautiful yellow creature circling freely around, and it seemed to him that there was something familiar about it. It was a butterfly and it had the loving eyes of Yellow.

He decided to clamber down, explaining to others he met that he wanted to become a butterfly. Finally he reached the bottom, tired and went to sleep. Yellow was there looking lovingly at him and indicating to him how he, too, could change into a beautiful butterfly.

Have I inside me the means not only to make cocoons but also the stuff of butterflies, too?

⋆ ⋆ ⋆

The papal preacher, Fr Raneiro Cantalmessa, said once that John Lennon's famous phrase, "Imagine there's no heaven," revealed an empty, secularised vision of man's destiny; and Fr Buzzetti, a Biblical scholar, suggested that the Church doesn't "sell" heaven, but makes it out to be dull and vague and boring and monotonous with an 'anaemic' atmosphere. The idea of an eternal banquet, repose, or the vision of God is not particularly attractive.

One problem is that of leaving behind those one loves most. But these relationships will continue to exist but will be transfigured, not nullified. Perhaps this life will be present in the next in a similar way that infancy is present in the life of an adult. The best way is to think of heaven as the love and happiness one feels when doing good. It is a relationship with God, the Trinity.

⋆ ⋆ ⋆

Bereavement is a suffering nearly all of us have to undergo at some time or other in our lives. On hearing of the death of a friend I had known and loved more than fifty years ago, but had only seen a few times since, I was surprised at the depth of feeling and emotion that I experienced. The news left me with an empty sadness and regret of things unsaid and experiences unshared.........until I reminded myself that through prayer and the Risen Lord's Presence we are close to those we love and who have gone before us.

⋆ ⋆ ⋆

'Master, what does it mean to be enlightened?'

'It means knowing that I am going to die.'

'But, Master, everybody knows they are going to die.'

'Ah yes, but not everybody lives with the knowledge.'

A recent study claims that people today do not mature until after thirty-five: living as if there is no tomorrow after death without giving thought to a final judgement and eternity. Maturity involves facing the facts of life.........and the fact of death which leads to the fullness of life in the next world.

⋆ ⋆ ⋆

Two embryos are chatting in their mother's womb:

- Do you believe in life after birth?
- Of course, There ought to be something after birth. Probably we are here to prepared for what comes after this state.

- Nonsense. There is nothing after birth. Anyway, what would it be like?
- I don't have a clue, but I think there will be more light than here. Maybe we'll walk on our feet and eat with our mouth.
- Rubbish! It's impossible to walk. And eat with your mouth? Really! We take nourishment through the umbilical cord. But I tell you something: life after death is impossible because the umbilical cord is already too short.
- But there must be something. Probably it'll be different from what we are used to.
- Nobody has returned from there. With birth life simply ends. Life is nothing more than always being cramped in the darkness.
- I don't know exactly what will happen, but we will see Mum and she will take care of us.
- Mum? Do you believe in Mum? Are you foolish? And where do you think she is?
- Everywhere. Around us. We live in her and because of her. We wouldn't exist at all without her.
- I doubt it! I have never ever seen any kind of Mum, so her non-existence is obvious.
- You know, sometimes when we are silent we can hear how she sings, or feel how she gently strokes the world around us. You know I truly believe that real life is ahead of us.

(source unknown)

CONCLUSION

The Church is, in many ways, like a family, and as in most families there can be disagreements. I love the Lord and I love his Church which he founded on Peter and the Apostles. There are times, however, when, like many of us, I become exasperated by certain things happening or being said – and I ask if this or that is really according to Christ's law of love.

As I write this I am concerned about the Church's discipline regarding celibacy of the clergy. There have always been married clergy under the umbrella of the Church, and there would seem to be no reason why this could not be extended, not as a complete answer to the shortage of priests, but as a help to alleviate the problem. I have been impressed by the wonderful example and way of life of some Eastern Rite Catholic priests, married with young families, whom I have met in Austria at the International Theological Institute for students on marriage and the family. This, together with the encouragement of priests to live in small communities, with committed lay people, would, as I see it, be an important way forward.

Then there is the whole question of the rightful place of women in the Church, and the first step might be the acceptance of women deacons.

If the way of life of the diocesan clergy does not radically change, then there will be fewer celebrations of the Eucharist, fewer priests to show compassion and give the Sacraments to those who are crying out for them; and this includes those remarried after a divorce or who are married to a divorcee. Are we going to continue to deprive them of the Sacraments? These and other problems are the concern of many of us, clergy and laity, in this great family to which we belong, the one Catholic Church.

However, to bring these notebook jottings to an end on a positive note, I am including yet another broadcast talk I gave on the radio in Cyprus in the late 1960s, and I think it is relevant here:

<u>Happiness is love that gives itself.</u>

Yesterday I ended by posing the question: how can we be really happy? And the answer is of course, by loving! You know, recently, a certain agnostic said: "One must want to be happy......The egoist is sad because he's waiting for happiness to come along, and instead, along comes boredom. On the contrary, good humour indicates generosity. It gives rather than receives. And it's true that we must think of the happiness of others; but, you know, one doesn't hear enough said about making those we love happy by being happy ourselves." And he adds: "It's a duty to others to be happy." Happiness is a sort of service we render to others – have you ever thought of it like that?

Oh yes, all that's O.K. you might be saying, but how can one be happy when there's so much physical and moral misery all around one? Has one any right to ooze out happiness when there are so many who are suffering and miserable, with a ghastly war going on in Vietnam, Africans in revolt, two thirds of the world undernourished, and so on.......? Evil and suffering are the result of sin. "There is for every sin, somewhere in the world and in time, a corresponding suffering", (Michael Quoist). Sin and suffering are evils, but for the Christian, evils with a purpose, for through our sufferings, God can accomplish his Redemption. We can then understand why the Easter liturgy describes the original sin of man as "a happy fault that gave rise to the coming of such a Saviour." God invariably brings good out of evil if we turn trustfully to him. It would certainly be wrong if in our own happy state we had no care for those in need. But if our "joie de vivre" has its source in the gift of self and the love of others, then we are right in testifying to this.

Happiness and love are very closely tied together. From time immemorial poets have talked about it, and whenever two of our friends get married, we send them a card and a present with the word – good wishes for your happiness. The whole history of man's quest after happiness is in fact the history of the ways in which he loves. But the reverse isn't necessarily true........All of you listening this morning, will, at some time or another, have watched a tiny child with its mother. The child tries to attract the attention of its mother. It does it by every means in its power: by smiles, by tears, cries, by breaking things, and so on, until she's compelled to leave all else and give her attention entirely to the child. Adults are sometimes like this child. Applied to an adult, to a free and conscious being, this is a possessive sort of love: a person who wants above all else to satisfy his or her desires, to use another person for his own satisfaction, to make of another a sort of object. This kind of love can lead to pleasure; but it's not sufficient to lead on to happiness. And yet it's often the case unfortunately between husband and wife. It's a sign of immaturity in love. Similarly, solitary acts of impurity are signs of immaturity, of a love-energy, of a quest for happiness that has not sufficiently developed.

The love of a mother, on the contrary, invariably involves the gift of self, of sacrifice. The mother gives herself to her child. Attentive to his or her slightest needs, she's ready to sacrifice her leisure, her sleep, and her strength. There are days when, tired, worn out, a mother will surpass herself, in order to satisfy the requirements of her love. But it's through doing this that she will find true joy; it's through this that she will find true happiness. Psychologists bear this out: an adult can only find joy, equilibrium, fulfilment of self if, in himself, this outward-turning love, as it were, outweighs the inward-turning.

Neither the wisdom of nations nor Christ himself, use any other language when they tell us that there is more joy in giving than in receiving. The way to happiness passes through the gift of self, the gift of love, because God is love and loves each one of us totally.

⋆ ⋆ ⋆

Happiness was seen in the faces of the 2008 Olympic athletes as they paraded around the Bird's Nest arena at the opening of the Beijing games. Coming from 204 different countries, they were giving themselves in the pursuit of sport, united in that aim; one world, one dream. Our destiny is also to be united through Jesus, the Way, the Truth and the Life in that deeper movement of love which is the Living God, the Trinity.

And so we are challenged to continue walking along the path of trust, building up small communities of reconciliation and love within the all embracing community of the Church. Let us always remember St Paul's words, "Nothing can ever come between us and the love of God revealed to us in Christ Jesus."

I conclude with one of my favourite prayers which I find impossible to pray with complete sincerity, but which I hope to be able to do before the Lord finally calls me.

Father, I abandon myself into your hands;
Do with me what you will.
Whatever you may do, I thank you:
I am ready for all, I accept all.
Let only your will be done in me,
And in all your creatures.
I wish no more than this, O Lord.
Into your hands I commend my soul;
I offer it to you with all the love of my heart,
For I love you, Lord, and so need to give myself,
To surrender myself into your hands,
Without reserve and with boundless confidence,
For you are my Father.

Also available from the same author

SHADES OF WELCOME (2002)
ISBN 978-184426-007-2

Available from all good booksellers or
www.upfrontpublishing.com

Also available from the same author

STRETCH OUT YOUR HAND (2005)
ISBN 978-184426-254-5

Available from all good booksellers or
www.upfrontpublishing.com

Also available from the same author

WHAT SHALL I SAY? (2005)
ISBN 978-185607-513-8

Available from all good booksellers or
www.columba.ie

Also available from the same author

Central Line To Eziat (2008)
ISBN 978-184426-461-2

Available from all good booksellers or
www.upfrontpublishing.com

ND - #0246 - 080726 - C0 - 198/129/15 - PB - 9781844265909 - Gloss Lamination